2 Miniature portrait of Beethoven on ivory (6·5 × 5·4 cm) by Christian Horneman, dated 1803.

BEETHOVEN

A Documentary Study
compiled and edited by
H. C. Robbins Landon

121 illustrations, 34 in colour

THAMES AND HUDSON · LONDON

Translated from the German by
RICHARD WADLEIGH and EUGENE HARTZELL

First published in Great Britain in 1970 by Thames and Hudson Ltd,
London, by arrangement with Universal Edition A.G., Zurich
This abridged edition published in 1974
© 1970 and 1974 Universal Edition A.G., Zurich

Printed and bound in Great Britain by Jarrold and Sons Ltd, Norwich

ISBN 0 500 18146 2 hardcover
ISBN 0 500 20140 4 paperback

Contents

1 Ludwig van Beethoven; anonymous
wax relief, attributed to J. N. Lang,
1815/18(?).

3 Silhouette portrait of the young
Beethoven, by Joseph Neesen, c. 1786.

4 Beethoven at the age of thirteen, an anonymous portrait rediscovered in 1972.

Introduction to a Beethoven Iconography

We owe the portrait, which, until very recently, was the earliest known likeness of Beethoven, to his friends, the Breuning family: a silhouette, showing the young composer at about the age of sixteen. The silhouette was first published in the *Biographische Notizen* by F. A. Wegeler and F. Ries in 1838, and the original is in a private collection in Vienna. The artist was one Joseph Neesen, possibly an amateur; in any case, he was very obscure and is known only for his silhouettes of Beethoven and the Breuning family; perhaps he was a friend of theirs.

If this early Beethoven portrait survives as something of a happy accident, another – an oil painting showing the composer at the age of thirteen – was rediscovered only in 1952 and has since been restored at the Historisches Museum of the City of Vienna. This anonymous painting was bought by a German doctor at an auction in Brunswick; it is a half-length portrait, 17 × 22 cm, inscribed on the back of the canvas 'L.H.' Beethoven as a 13-year-old. Gift of Beethoven to Baron von Smeskal [Zmeskall; see p. 51]'. Although there is little doubt that the painting dates from the late eighteenth century, examinations have shown that another inscription on the back of the canvas – 'L. van Beethoven' – is later than the one already referred to, and that some changes have been made around the mouth and chin. All that is known about the painting's provenance is that it had been in the possession of Dr Klamann-Parlo, an art collector from Silesia, who died in 1966.

The third portrait, chronologically, owes its existence to the composer's rapidly growing fame in Vienna at the turn of the century. It is an engraving published in 1800 by Giovanni Cappi, formerly a business partner in the famous house of Artaria & Co. In a letter to Wegeler of 19 January 1801, Beethoven refers to the publisher as Artaria; either Artaria issued it first and later passed it on to Cappi when the latter founded his own business, or Beethoven still thought of Cappi as part of the Artaria establishment. The print is based on a design by Gandolph Ernst Stainhauser von Treuberg, and was engraved by Johann Neidl, who often worked for Artaria (he engraved, for instance, the portrait of Haydn based on the Zitterer painting). Neither Stainhauser nor Neidl is an artist of the first rank, but we can gain through the engraving our first impression of Beethoven as a famous young man in Vienna at the turn of the century: wavy dark hair; sideburns; a serious, rather full face; elegant clothing of the period. The engraving was presumably copied in Leipzig, without naming the artist; it was issued there by Beethoven's

5 A somewhat idealized portrait by Joseph Willibrord Mähler, painted about 1804 or 1805. Beethoven kept this painting on his wall until he died.

friend and brother-Mason Franz Anton Hoffmeister at his 'Bureau de Musique' in 1801. That Beethoven was an interesting subject to artists even at this relatively early date is clear from a passage in a letter to Christine Gerhardi, undated but evidently written in the 1790s, in which he refers to a portrait issued without his knowledge.★

The first really good Beethoven portrait is the beautiful miniature signed and dated 1803 by Christian Horneman, the Danish artist who worked in Berlin and then came to Vienna about 1798 with a letter of recommendation to the famous portraitist, Johann Heinrich Füger. Many of Horneman's miniatures have been preserved, including portraits of King Friedrich Wilhelm III and Queen Luise of Prussia as well as Joseph Haydn (the latter reproduced by Karl Geiringer, 1932, in his *Joseph Haydn*). Beethoven gave the miniature to his friend Stephan von Breuning, and it remained in the Breuning family for more than a hundred years before passing to the famous Beethoven collector, Dr H. C. Bodmer, and from him to the Beethovenhaus in Bonn. Comparison with the Klein mask (see below) shows that Horneman accurately represented Beethoven's facial features and proportions – even to the disfiguring pock-marks – except, perhaps, the nose. There is no doubt, however, that the Horneman miniature is the most important Beethoven portrait before the life-mask of 1812.

The dapper Beethoven of this period is not, incidentally, a figment of these artists' flattering imagination: we have corroborative evidence from no less a figure than the Austrian playwright Franz Grillparzer, who met the composer about 1804 or 1805 and later described him, 'contrary to his later habits', as being most elegantly dressed. A life-size painting of about this period shows us a slightly idealized but none the less interesting portrait of the composer: the artist was Joseph Willibrord Mähler, a fellow countryman of Beethoven's from the Rhineland, who although an amateur, gained a considerable reputation as a portraitist of musicians. Mähler appears to have been a friend of Beethoven's, and we may therefore assume that the composer actually sat for the portrait; it remained in Beethoven's possession till his death. Some ten years ago, it was cleaned and expertly restored by the Historisches Museum of the

★ Dear Chr[istine], ·   [Vienna, 1797]
You said something yesterday about that likeness of me – I do wish that in this matter you would proceed rather circumspectly. For I fear that if we choose F. to return it, perhaps that wretched B. or that extremely stupid Joseph will interfere and, in that case, the affair may then become a trick to be played upon me; and that would be really deplorable. I should have to revenge myself again; and surely the whole populace don't deserve that. Try to get hold of the thing, if it is at all possible to do so. I assure you that after this experience I will appeal in the Press to all painters not to paint me again without my knowledge. I really did not think that this face of mine would ever cause me embarrassment. . . .   (Emily Anderson, *Letters of Beethoven*, London 1961, I, 29.)

City of Vienna, to which it now belongs. A careful comparison with the 1812 life-mask shows the general features to be for the most part accurate, though, as said above, idealized. An undated note from Beethoven to Mähler refers to this portrait: 'I beg you to return my portrait to me as soon as you have made sufficient use of it – if you need it longer I beg of you at least to make haste – I have promised the portrait to a stranger, a lady who saw it here, that she may hang it in her room during her stay of several weeks. Who can withstand such *charming importunities*, as a matter of course a portion of the lovely favours *which I shall thus garner* will also fall to *you*.'★

The great Beethoven scholar A. W. Thayer spoke with Mähler (who did not die till 1860) about this portrait:★★ 'To the question what picture is here referred to, Mr Mähler replied to the author [Thayer] in substance: "It was a portrait, which I painted soon after coming to Vienna, in which Beethoven is represented, at nearly full length, sitting; the left hand rests upon a lyre, the right is extended, as if, in a moment of musical enthusiasm, he was beating time; in the background is a temple of Apollo. Oh! If I could but know what became of the picture!"

'"What!" was the author's answer, to the great satisfaction of the old gentleman, "the picture is hanging at this moment in the home of Madame van Beethoven, widow, in the Josephstadt, and I have a copy of it."'

Thayer's copy, which has been widely reproduced, is now in the New York Public Library.

The next portrait to follow the Mähler painting is that of Isidor Neugass, who had just before [1805/6] painted the rather ugly, but by no means unrealistic, portrait of Haydn holding a sheet of the *Creation* in his hand (Eisenstadt Castle: reproduced in László Somfai, *Joseph Haydn, Sein Leben in zeitgenössischen Bildern*, Kassel-Basel-Paris-London 1966, p. 201). Two versions of the Neugass painting are known. The one which is probably the original is signed 'peinte par Neugass Wienne 1806'; it was commissioned by Prince Carl Lichnowsky, and hung for many years in Grätz Castle, Lichnowsky's country estate. It is still in the family's possession and is now in South America. The other, now in Paris, is the so-called 'Brunsvik portrait'; it was formerly in one of the Brunsviks' castles, either Korompa or Márton Vasár. Theodor von Frimmel, the great Beethoven scholar, was able to prove that Neugass himself executed the 'Brunsvik portrait', even though it is not signed or

★ *Thayer's Life of Beethoven* (ed. by Elliot Forbes), Princeton 1967, I, 337. See also Anderson I, 125.
★★ *Ibid.*

6 Beethoven in about 1806; portrait in oils by Isidor Neugass. Another signed and dated Neugass portrait was formerly owned by Prince Lichnowsky in Grätz Castle and is now in the possession of Lichnowsky descendants in South America.

dated. In his *Beethoven-Handbuch* (I, 43) Frimmel quotes a letter from Therese von Brunsvik to her brother dated 1807: 'During the last few days I have seen a lot of Beethoven. . . . A certain Neigart has painted him and has the portrait in his studio.' Therese meant, of course, Neugass; in this same letter, she says the portrait is to be sent to her sister Josephine. In later years, the Neugass 'Brunsvik portrait' was in Florence; it is now in private possession in Paris. Neugass is not a first-rate artist, and his Beethoven portraits are rather stylized, but they are useful, as any authentic iconographic documentation of Beethoven must be. Note, for example, the chain round the neck which obviously carried Beethoven's double lorgnette (Grillparzer noted that in 1804–05 Beethoven wore spectacles when reading); even at this relatively early period, he was not only hard of hearing, but also short-sighted. Note, also, the almost foppish elegance of Beethoven's clothing and general appearance.

Beethoven at the period of the *Fifth Symphony* is shown to us in an amusing pencil sketch by an artist who was very famous at the time, Ludwig Ferdinand Schnorr von Carolsfeld.* The drawing, done in a

---

* Otto Erich Deutsch, in his article 'Beethovens Leben in Bildern' (*Österreichische Musikzeitschrift*, 16. Jahrgang, Heft 3, March 1961), suggests that not Ludwig but his father Johann Veit (Veit Hans) von Carolsfeld is the author of the sketch.

sketchbook of Beethoven's friends, the Malfatti family, is dated 'about 1808 or 1809' in a note written on the same page. Though hastily executed, the drawing is very faithful to Beethoven's features and lively – rather like a snapshot today.

Without any question, the most important documentary evidence of Beethoven's features is the life-mask made by the Austrian sculptor Franz Klein in 1812, as well as the bust prepared by Klein on the basis of that mask. Theodor von Frimmel was able to learn some hitherto unknown facts about the mask from descendants of the Streicher family, for it was evidently the piano manufacturer Andreas Streicher who commissioned Klein to make the mask. Klein's first attempt failed – Beethoven thought he would suffocate under the wet gypsum. The bust is therefore especially valuable because of its realistic portrayal of Beethoven's hair – something which was naturally missing from the facial mask. On the other hand, the mask preserves with complete accuracy the proportions of Beethoven's face, even to the ugly pock-marks and scars.

The spectacular success of Beethoven's *Battle at Vittoria* and the charity concerts of 1814 were no doubt responsible for a new engraving of the composer, since the engraved portrait issued in 1800 was by now out of date. Fortunately A. W. Thayer found Blasius Höfel, the engraver of the new print, still alive in 1860, and was able to learn from him the facts surrounding the new portrait. Artaria – still one of Beethoven's principal publishers – had engaged the fashionable French artist Louis Letronne to make a drawing of Beethoven as the basis for a new engraving. Blasius Höfel, then a young man at the beginning of his career, found the drawing unsatisfactory and requested Beethoven to sit again for him; the composer agreed and Höfel refashioned the drawing. Contemporaries agreed that it was an excellent portrait: Aloys Fuchs, the great Viennese music collector, said to Thayer: 'Thus I learned to know him [Beethoven]', obviously a very literal translation of '*So* habe ich ihn kennengelernt'. Nevertheless the engraving of 1814 is somewhat idealized: there are no pock-marks, for instance. What makes the engraving interesting is the undeniable impression of strength which seems to jump out from the face on the printed page. Recently, what purports to be the original Letronne drawing has come to light in Paris; it is not so bad as its reputation, but it does make Beethoven rather a French dandy. Beethoven himself sent a good many copies of the engraving to his friends. One, quoted by Frimmel (*Beethoven-Handbuch*, I, 219), was sent to Antonia von Brentano, and an autograph inscription on it reads: 'Hochachtungsvoll der Frau Von Brentano gebohren Edle Von Birken-

stock von ihrem Sie verehrenden Freund Beethoven'. Höfel, who was some twenty-two years old in 1814, became very successful as a result of the Beethoven engraving. The Thieme-Becker *Allgemeines Künstler-Lexikon* (XVII, 1924) writes of it: 'Höfel's first engraving, which made him famous and brought him many commissions, was the excellent Beethoven portrait after Louis Letronne.'

Beethoven's fame at the time of the Congress of Vienna provided the occasion for several other portraits. One is Mähler's second attempt to paint the composer. The portrait exists in at least three versions, of which the finest – recently cleaned by the Historisches Museum of the City of Vienna – is owned by Wolfgang von Karajan in Salzburg. Of the others, the Gesellschaft der Musikfreunde copy has a curiously lifeless appearance with rather cold eyes, while the third was made for Beethoven's friend Ignaz von Gleichenstein and sent to Germany; this 'German' version is still owned by the Gleichenstein family. The Gesellschaft der Musik-freunde version has been widely reproduced, the others less so. On the whole, the second Mähler portrait – which was first mentioned in a report dated August 1815 – is not entirely satisfactory. The proportions of the face are not exact if we compare them to the Klein mask of 1812,

7 Pencil portrait of Beethoven by Louis Letronne, presumed to have been executed in 1814, though dated 1821.

8 Beethoven is said to have sat for this pencil drawing by Gustav Adolph Hippius, made between 1814 and 1816, when Hippius was in Vienna.

and the painter has certainly not caught the composer's 'inner life' on the canvas. Nevertheless it does not deserve the rather casual dismissal it receives from Frimmel (*Beethoven-Handbuch*, I, 44).

The best thing about another portrait supposedly executed in 1815, that of Johann Christoph Heckel, is – as opposed to Mähler's – the expression. It shows the same stubborn, rebellious and square-jawed Beethoven that we know to be truthful from the Klein mask and which has been rendered famous through the Waldmüller painting of 1823. The Heckel portrait, for which Beethoven sat at Streicher's piano rooms, was in private possession for many years and was last owned by the Lehman family, who gave it to the Library of Congress. Heckel's conception of the lower part of Beethoven's face is not entirely accurate.

Another Beethoven portrait from the period of the Vienna Congress is a pencil sketch by Gustav Adolph Hippius, who was in Vienna during the years 1814 to 1816. In some respects, the Hippius sketch may be profitably compared to the earlier pencil drawing of 1808: neither is great art nor even great portraiture, but each contains a certain liveliness. The Hippius sketch remained unknown until its discovery in Russia and subsequent publication by Theodor von Frimmel.

9 Another Mähler portrait (see ill. 5), which can be dated to about August 1815.

10 Beethoven in 1815; a dated portrait by Johann Christoph Heckel.

11 Portrait by Ferdinand Schimon, painted in 1818 or 1819, when Beethoven was immersed in work on his *Missa Solemnis*.

12 A strongly idealized portrait by Joseph Carl Stieler, 1819–20.

The well-known German artist August Carl Friedrich von Kloeber painted Beethoven at Mödling in 1818. The circumstances are related below, in the documents. Unfortunately the big painting – of which a very detailed contemporary description survives,[*] and which also included Beethoven's nephew Carl, sleeping under a tree – has long disappeared. We have three preliminary sketches, of which we reproduce the one showing the composer's head. Although very famous, and often reproduced, the Kloeber sketches are not very impressive. The hair is obviously well done, but the features are, once again, not entirely accurate and the expression is curiously lacking in feeling. Part of the difficulty which most artists found when drawing or painting Beethoven seems to have been due to the fact that the composer was impatient and would not sit still for long. Some of the Beethoven portraits were done under highly unfavourable circumstances, and sections later completed from memory. Conversely, some artists managed not to disturb Beethoven and did their work while he was composing or improvising at the piano (e.g. Blasius Höfel and, later, Schimon).

In the autumn of 1818, a young Austro-Hungarian artist, Ferdinand Schimon, a pupil of Lampi the younger, painted Beethoven's portrait. It has since become very famous and is certainly one of the most interesting and persuasive of all the known oil portraits of the composer. Felix Anton Schindler, Beethoven's friend and biographer, considered it the most interesting, and relates in detail how the portrait came into existence. He writes:[**] 'From an artistic point of view Schimon's work is not a distinguished work of art, yet full of characteristic truth. In the rendering of that particular look, the majestic forehead, this dwelling-place of mighty, sublime ideas, of hues, in the drawing of the firmly shut mouth and the chin shaped like a shell, it is truer to nature than any other picture.' Schindler owned the portrait which, he later reports, 'has unfortunately darkened greatly'; it went to the Royal Prussian (later State) Library and is now in the Beethovenhaus in Bonn. The composer, incidentally, was satisfied with Schimon's work.

Equally notable, and as often reproduced as the Schimon portrait, is the famous picture made in 1819 by the Munich artist Joseph Carl Stieler; the portrait is signed and dated 1819 but was not in fact completed until the next year. Contemporaries, including Schindler, thought it a good likeness, though the hands were completed from memory.

---

[*] *Wiener Zeitschrift für Kunst, Literatur und Mode*, 1818, p. 1134. Quoted *in extenso* in Frimmel's *Beethoven-Handbuch*, I, 280.

[**] Translation from *Thayer's Life of Beethoven*, op. cit., II, 742.

Stieler was a clever diplomat and managed to persuade the composer to sit for him three times – something of a feat for anyone. The conversation books contain several entries in Stieler's hand, e.g. (December 1819 or January 1820): 'Setzen Sie sich doch gefälligst, als wenn Sie schreiben, um die Stellung zu probieren. . . . Wenn ich Ihnen winke, bitte in der Stellung zu bleiben, die Sie gerade haben.'* Some further extracts are cited below, in the documents. Astute observers will notice a considerable difference in the Beethoven of Schimon and that of Stieler. Schindler explains it by saying that 'the startling difference . . . is the result of the long illness that had intervened'.** The best thing about the portrait is undoubtedly the 'thoughtful expression' (Frimmel). In 1826, Mathias Artaria published a lithograph of the Stieler portrait by the artist's nephew Friedrich Dürck. Later the famous artist Joseph Kriehuber made a lithograph based on the Stieler portrait. The original oil painting is owned by Walter Hinrichsen in New York City.

Joseph Daniel Böhm, a young artist and engraver, managed to persuade Beethoven to sit at least once – possibly twice. We find an entry in one of the conversation books of 1820: 'Der Böhm wünscht, dass Sie ihm noch eine Sitzung schenken möchten',*** but we do not know if the answer was yes or no. Böhm made two sketches of Beethoven walking – the originals are now in the Beethovenhaus – and later he himself prepared silver plates of these sketches; copies of the silver plate versions, which are signed with Böhm's initials, are owned by André Meyer in Paris. Böhm also intended to strike a medal of Beethoven, and for this purpose prepared a wax medallion: a rather dim copy, made by Frimmel, was given to the Beethovenhaus, but the original has disappeared.

At this period it became fashionable to do sketches of the famous Beethoven on his walks. Quite a number of these interesting sketches have been preserved, some contemporary and some apparently posthumous. Martin Tejček is supposed to have observed Beethoven walking, and his sketch was used as the basis for a lithograph issued at Prague in 1841: it is useful primarily for its detailed view of Beethoven's clothing. Another drawing, the original of which has disappeared, is an amusing and realistic picture of Beethoven walking in the pouring rain, the collar

---

* Please sit as if you were writing, so as to try out the position. . . . When I wave to you, please remain in the very position you are in.' W. Nohl's edition of the conversation books, I, 327, 336.

** Schindler: *Beethoven As I Knew Him*, edited by Donald W. MacArdle, Chapel Hill and London 1966, p. 451. Throughout this present book we have gratefully used the MacArdle edition but have always done our own translations or, occasionally, used those in *Thayer's Life of Beethoven*.

*** 'Böhm wishes that you would sit for him once more'. See Frimmel, *Beethoven-Handbuch*, I, 53.

of his greatcoat turned up against the wind: the original was a water-coloured pen-and-ink drawing by Johann Nepomuk Hoechle. Joseph Weidner, who supposedly made a portrait of the composer in oils, fashioned a characteristic sketch of Beethoven *a tergo*, brandishing a walking stick and lost to the world: it is one of the best of these sketches, which were undoubtedly made without Beethoven's knowledge.

Recently an interesting wax relief of Beethoven was discovered in Vienna, together with reliefs – apparently by the same hand – of other popular figures such as the Emperor Franz I, the Empress Caroline Augusta and Nicolò Paganini. This small but interesting collection belongs to the Historisches Museum of the City of Vienna, and in a recent publication Franz Glück, former Director of the Museum, was able to ascribe all these wax reliefs with confidence to the rather obscure artist Joseph Nikolaus Lang (1776–1835). Lang also made a medal to commemorate Beethoven's death in 1827.[*] Obviously the wax relief is the model for the medal, but, as Glück points out, the relief is much finer artistically and it was probably made during the composer's life-time. Glück dates the relief 1815–1818 (*op. cit.*, p. 209) and we have no reason to dispute this tentative dating.

It is interesting that young artists – like young people in general – were attracted to Beethoven. Another promising Austrian artist was the sculptor Anton Dietrich, for whom Beethoven sat in 1819–1820, when the artist was just turned twenty-one. Dietrich also took Klein's life-mask as the model for his bust, which was first shown in 1820. Dietrich made at least half a dozen copies, including life-size ones, some of them dated 1821 (one such variant is illustrated here); later he did a not very realistic drawing. The Dietrich busts, judged *in toto*, are accurately proportioned but highly idealized and slightly cold. Franz Glück, in the interesting article mentioned above, also discusses the Dietrich busts at some length. Since Frimmel wrote about them the five Dietrich busts known at that time have all, except for the one owned by the Historisches Museum of the City of Vienna, disappeared from sight. From extant photographs, Glück was able to show that there seem to be two basic versions which Dietrich made: of the first, the museum owns a version of 1821; of the other, rather more formal bust *à l'antique*, no copy seems to exist at present. Glück considers, and we beg leave to concur, that the Museum version, with its strong jaw and the realistic portrayal of the hair,

* Franz Glück *Prolegomena zu einer neuen Beethoven-Ikonographie*, Festschrift Otto Erich Deutsch zum 80. Geburtstag am 5. September 1963, hrsg. von Walter Gerstenberg, Jan LaRue und Wolfgang Rehm, Kassel, Basel, Paris, London, New York 1963. Photograph after p. 208.

13 Portrait of Beethoven by
Ferdinand Georg
Waldmüller, 1823.

is the better of the two *Ur*-versions. Glück was also able to make an important discovery in the identification of the document quoted in connection with this bust.

In 1823, when Beethoven was particularly irritable, the great Austrian painter Ferdinand Georg Waldmüller was commissioned by Breitkopf & Härtel in Leipzig to do a portrait of the composer. The unfavourable circumstances in which this portrait was painted are described below, in the documentary section. It led Schindler to a sweeping denunciation of the Waldmüller painting, after quoting the document in question, Schindler continues:

'In a word, the Waldmüller portrait is, if possible, further from the truth than any other. It is the likeness of a venerable pastor whose thoughts are occupied with elaborating a homily for the edification of his congregation. Even in its outlines, it has nothing in common with the head of Beethoven, the composer in whose mind there was evolving at that time the Ninth Symphony.'★

★ Schindler, *op. cit.*, p. 454.

But Waldmüller was by far the greatest artist ever to paint Beethoven, and his work cannot be dismissed so lightly. Theodor von Frimmel, writing of the portrait, says:

'Nevertheless it is a highly valuable document which presents us a Beethoven as he "growls and scowls". Waldmüller's quite exceptional memory for shapes has given us, in any event, something more valuable than small talents with days of effort.'*

The original oil painting in the offices of Breitkopf & Härtel was destroyed during World War II, but a colour photograph exists. At least one authentic copy by Waldmüller has survived.

Beethoven, a few days after the first performance of the *Ninth Symphony*, is shown to us in the idealistic chalk drawing by Stephan Decker (May 1824), of which a lithograph was published in the *Wiener Allgemeine Musikalische Zeitung* on 5 June 1824 (wherein Decker's drawing is also mentioned as having been made 'a few days' after the famous concert). Beethoven looks grey and rather forbidding, but the master obviously approved of the lithograph because he occasionally presented one with a personal inscription. On 4 September 1825, when the composer was taking the cure at Baden, he dedicated a Decker lithograph to the publisher Moritz Adolf Schlesinger.** As far as can now be determined, Decker's is the last portrait of Beethoven before the composer lay on his deathbed.

The well-known portraitist Joseph Teltscher, a member of the Schubert circle, made three drawings of Beethoven on his deathbed (one, of the bed only without Beethoven, has been omitted from our illustrations) – profoundly moving documents of the dying man, his body beneath the bed-clothes swollen with dropsy. Theodor von Frimmel discovered these fascinating drawings in the famous collection of Dr August Heymann in Vienna, and published them for the first time in May 1909. They were later in the Stefan Zweig collection and are now owned by Zweig's heir, Mrs Eva Alberman.

Tragic in a curiously impersonal, objective way – quite unlike the pathetic and terribly private sketches by Teltscher – is the sketch of Beethoven in death made on 28 March 1827 (the day after his death) by Joseph Danhauser – again, another young artist making a pilgrimage to the great composer. (Teltscher, too, was young: he was born in 1802, Danhauser in 1805.) Danhauser published a lithograph of the drawing. He also made the famous death-mask, which, it was hitherto believed,

* *Beethoven-Handbuch*, I, 46.
** *Beethoven-Handbuch*, I, 47.

showed the composer horribly disfigured by the autopsy which had been made before Danhauser could begin his work. Beethoven's organs of hearing were removed for study, and to facilitate this the temporal bones had to be sawed out, thus causing the facial muscles to 'sag'. Franz Glück, in the article about Beethoven iconography quoted before, uncovered a document concerning the death-mask which seems to have escaped the notice of Beethoven scholars. It is a letter by Carl Danhauser, Joseph's brother, and it seems to suggest that the mask and drawing may both have been done before the autopsy, and in any case very early in the morning of 28 March 1827. This document is perhaps not precise evidence as to whether the autopsy had in fact been made or not: the subject is not specifically mentioned. On the other hand, other contemporaries are careful to state that Danhauser did not begin his work until the autopsy was finished. What is perhaps of vital importance to us is the condition of the death-mask itself. Glück is quite correct in pointing out that it is not nearly the second-rate document it has frequently been described to be, and that most writers – including to a certain extent Frimmel – have concentrated on the third- or fourth-hand copy in the Beethovenhaus in Bonn rather than on the superb cast from Franz Liszt's collection, now owned by the Historisches Museum of the City of Vienna, and here reproduced in profile. As Glück concludes: 'On the basis of the death-mask, we would know him, this great man, even if we did not know whom it represents.'

14 Beethoven's death-mask, by Joseph Danhauser.

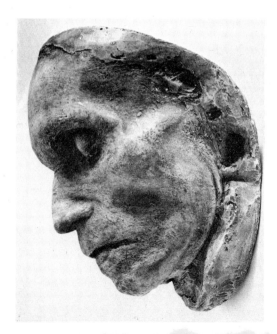

Abbreviations of Sources

Anderson — Emily Anderson, *The Letters of Beethoven*, London 1961, 3 vols.

Breuning — Gerhard von Breuning, *Aus dem Schwarzspanierhaus*, Vienna 1874.

Czerny — Carl Czerny, *Über den richtigen Vortrag der sämtlichen Beethoven'schen Klavierwerke sowie das 2. und 3. Kapitel des IV. Bandes der vollständigen theoretisch-praktischen Pianoforte-Schule Op. 500.* Edited and revised by Paul Badura-Skoda, Vienna 1963. (Wiener Urtext Ausgabe.)

Du Montet — Baronne du Montet, *Souvenirs 1785–1866,* Paris 1914. (German version, *Die Erinnerungen der Baronin Du Montet,* translated by Ernst Klarwill, Zürich 1925.)

FRBS — Theodor von Frimmel, *Beethoven Studien,* Leipzig 1905–06, 2 vols.

HJB II — Haydn Yearbook II, 1963/64. E. Olleson, *Haydn in the diaries of Count Zinzendorf,* Vienna 1964.

HJB III — Haydn Yearbook III, 1965. E. Olleson, *Georg August Griesinger's correspondence with Breitkopf und Härtel,* Vienna 1965.

HJB V — Haydn Yearbook V, 1968. Else Radant, *The diaries of Joseph Carl Rosenbaum,* Vienna 1968.

Hist. Tb. — *Historisches Taschenbuch. Mit besonderer Hinsicht auf die Oesterreichischen Staaten. Geschichte des. 19. Jahrhunderts,* Vienna 1805–09, 3 vols.

KAL — Alfred Chr. Kalischer, *Beethovens sämtliche Briefe,* Berlin 1909, vol. I.

KFR — Kalischer-Frimmel, vol. II of Kalischer's edition of Beethoven's letters, revised by Theodor von Frimmel, Berlin 1910.

Kerst — Friedrich Kerst, *Die Erinnerungen an Beethoven,* Stuttgart 1913, 2 vols.

(Kerst is a compilation of material from original sources, some of which is derived from unpublished documents, letters, diaries, etc. These are given, as well as Kerst references.)

KHV — Georg Kinsky, *Das Werk Beethovens. Thematisch bibliographisches Verzeichnis seiner sämtlichen vollendeten Kompositionen,* completed and edited after the author's death by Hans Halm, Munich 1955.

Konv. N. — Walter Nohl, *Ludwig van Beethoven, Konversationshefte,* first half-volume, Munich 1924.

Konv. Sch. — Georg Schünemann, *Ludwig van Beethovens Konversationshefte,* vol. 2, Books XI–XXII, Berlin 1942.

Reichardt — Johann Friedrich Reichardt, *Vertraute Briefe, geschrieben auf einer Reise nach Wien, Ende 1808 und Anfang 1809,* edited by Gustav Gugitz, Munich 1915, 2 vols.

Schindler — Anton Schindler. *Ludwig van Beethoven,* fifth edition, newly edited by Fritz Volbach, Münster 1927.

Sonneck — O. G. Sonneck, *Beethoven Letters in America,* New York 1927.

TDR — Alexander Wheelock Thayer, *Ludwig van Beethovens Leben,* von Hermann Deiters neubearbeitet und von Hugo Riemann ergänzt, Leipzig 1901–11, 5 vols. (This biography was originally written in English, but the first edition appeared in a German version by Deiters.)

Thürheim — Countess Lulu Thürheim, *Mein Leben,* edited by René van Rhyn, Zürich 1923, 4 vols.

WRBN — Dr F. G. Wegeler and Ferdinand Ries, *Biographische Notizen über Beethoven,* Coblenz 1838.

Works of Beethoven are identified according to KHV (see above); WoO means *Werk ohne Opuszahl* (Work without Opus number).

Bonn was a pretty provincial town and the seat of the Archbishop and Elector of Cologne. Ludwig van Beethoven was born there, probably on 15 December 1770 (he was christened on 17 December but he always considered the 15th his birthday), the son of Johann van Beethoven and Maria Magdalena née Keverich. Johann was a tenor in the Court Kapelle, and Ludwig's grandfather, the Kapellmeister at Bonn, who also bore the name Ludwig or Louis, was still alive when the composer was born: he died in 1773 and Beethoven revered his memory throughout his life, keeping his portrait on his wall in Vienna. At the time Beethoven was born, the Elector and Archbishop of Cologne was Maximilian Friedrich, Count of Königsegg-Aulendorf, who was succeeded, in 1784, by Maximilian Franz, youngest brother of the Emperor Joseph II. Among Beethoven's earliest friends were the families of von Breuning and Wegeler. Members of both families later published their memoirs about Beethoven, which are of particular importance for the Bonn period in Beethoven's life.

Descriptions of Bonn by Thomas Pennant [English original]:

July 2
The country is much the same as far as an isle with a convent called Neuwied. On each side of the Rhine the hills increase in height, terminate in conic shapes, and on the tops of three are ruined castles composed of lofty slender towers. From this place the left shore is quite flat, that on the right continues till near opposite Bonne.

15 Arrival of Maximilian Franz, Archduke of Austria, in Bonn, 1780 (artist: F.J. Roussaux).

Landed there about seven o'clock. The palace makes a fine figure from the water, having a most extensive front. The town is large, the streets narrow and ill built, the fortifications strong but seem to have been long in a pacific state – the ditches being fruitful gardens and the ramparts covered with vines.

The Elector's palace is adjacent, a very large white pile, seemingly built at several times. The staircase is very handsome, cased with a mock marble and well stuccoed; the ceiling is exceedingly well painted, the subject Phoebus and several of his attendants that are made to float very lightly.

Thomas Pennant, *Tour on the Continent 1765*, London 1948, p. 145.

The Fischer manuscript:

Every year, on Saint Magdalen's day, the name and birthday of Madame van Beethoven would be celebrated festively. The music stands would be brought out of the *Tucksaal* [correctly *Doxal*, a room in the church adjoining the organ: in the Bonn church it was located on the right above the choir; the chairs and music-stands were stored there]. The chairs would then be placed right and left in the rooms facing the street and a canopy set up in the room where the portrait of Grandfather Ludwig van Beethoven hung, and handsomely decorated with flowers, laurel branches and foliage. Early in the evening Madame van Beethoven would be requested to retire betimes, and by ten o'clock everyone would be assembled and ready in the most complete silence. The tuning up would now begin and Madame van Beethoven would be awakened. She would then dress and be led in and seated on a beautifully decorated chair under the canopy. At that very moment magnificent music would strike up, resounding throughout the whole neighbourhood so that everyone who was preparing to go to bed became gay and cheerful. When the music ended a meal would be served up and the company ate and drank until those who had become light-headed and wished to dance would take off their shoes and dance in their stockinged feet in order not to make a commotion in the house. In this fashion the celebration would come to an end.

When Ludwig van Beethoven had become a little older he went to the teacher Huppert [presumably Rupert] in the elementary school in the Neustrasse [Neugasse] which runs into the Rheinstrasse, at number 1091. Later he went to the Cathedral school. According to his father, he did not learn very much at school; that is why his father so early seated

16 Beethoven's grandfather, Ludwig van Beethoven (1712–73); portrait in oils by Leopold Radoux. Born in Antwerp, he was the first musician in the family; when he moved to Bonn he became Kapellmeister of the Elector's Court.

him at the clavier and kept him at it so severely. Cäcilia Fischer related that when his father led him to the clavier he had to stand on a small bench to play. Oberbürgermeister Windeck also saw this. . . . Ludwig van Beethoven also received daily instruction on the violin. Once he happened to be playing without notes when his father came in and said 'What is all that silly nonsense you are scraping away so badly? You know that I cannot stand it. Scrape from notes, otherwise all your scraping will not be of any use to you.' When Johann van Beethoven received an unexpected visitor and Ludwig happened to come into the room, he would generally walk around the clavier and press down the keys with his right hand. Then his father would say 'What are you splashing there again; go away or I'll box your ears.' His father finally paid attention to him when he heard him play the violin; he was again playing out of his head without notes. His father said 'Don't you ever stop doing that in spite of what I have told you.' The boy went on playing and said to his father, 'But isn't that beautiful?' His father replied, 'That is another matter. You are not ready to play things out of your head. Work hard at the clavier and on the violin. Play the notes correctly; that is more important. When you have become good enough, then you can and will have to work out of your head hard enough.' Ludwig van Beethoven later also received daily lessons on the viola.

TDR I, 132, 426. (Beethoven's parents lived in the Fischer family's house. Beethoven also grew up there. Later the Fischer's son wrote his reminiscenes of Beethoven.)

The Fischer manuscript:

In the year 1776, Madame van Beethoven allowed herself to be persuaded by the Court musician Brandt to move to his house on the Neugasse (992), where she would have been closer to the Court, to the market and to the church. But this did not suit Johann van Beethoven; he was afraid that he would not be able to accommodate his belongings there. Moreover he thought that the outlook onto the wall of the Franciscan monastery was too gloomy. After the great fire of the palace in 1777, Beethoven feared for his home and went weeping to the Fischers. Since the apartment was vacant, the family moved there. Beethoven's children were happy and said, 'It is a good thing that we are here again; in the Rhine there is enough water to put out a fire.'

TDR I, 427.

The Fischer manuscript:

At Christmas time when the Elector, as Bishop, celebrated Mass in the Court chapel, from 11 to 12 midnight, the musicians and the Court Choir ladies in the Court *Tucksaal* had to give proof of their best strength and ability. All the Court nobility and servants attended in gala dress. The Electoral bodyguard lined each side in parade uniform, the entire regiment from the Koblenzer gate to the Palace chapel in full dress. After the first Gospel, half-way through the Mass and also after the last Gospel, they would fire three volleys followed by the cannon on the city ramparts. At this season it was often very cold. After the celebration, when Beethoven and his family with other friends had arrived home, following an old custom, they broiled fresh sausages and drank hot wine, punch and coffee. In this way, Christmas Eve would be celebrated and come to an end.

When Herr Johann van Beethoven had to sing in the Court *Tucksaal* he would suck a fresh raw egg or eat two prunes, on the morning before. He recommended this as being good for the voice.

Court musicians in gala dress. [Ludwig van Beethoven's attire]: sea-green tail coat, short green knee-breeches with buckles, white or black silk hose, shoes with black bows, a white flowered silk waistcoat with flap pockets, the waistcoat bordered with pure gold cord, hair dressed in curls and pigtail, a cocked hat under his left arm and a sword, carried also on the left, with a silver sword belt.

TDR I, 432, 429, 434.

17 Maximilian Friedrich, Elector and Arch-bishop of Cologne (1708–84), who engaged Beethoven's grandfather as Kapellmeister (anonymous portrait).

18 Maximilian Franz, youngest brother of the Emperor Joseph II, succeeded Maximilian Fried-rich as Elector of Cologne (anonymous portrait).

Wolfgang Amadeus Mozart writes to his father on 17 November 1781, about Maximilian Franz:

When God grants an office, He also grants understanding. And this is truly the case with the Archduke. Before he became a priest he was much more witty and clever, talked less but more sensibly. You should see him now! Stupidity peeks out from his eyes, he talks and speaks without ceasing and everything in a falsetto. He has a swelling in his throat. In a word, it is as if the man had changed completely.

TDR I, 161.

Dr Franz Gerhard Wegeler about Bonn:

Altogether it was a wonderful and in many ways an exciting time in Bonn as long as it was under the rule of the personally brilliant Elector Max Franz, Maria Theresa's youngest and favourite son.

TDR I, 162. (Dr Wegeler was Beethoven's friend in youth and later married Eleonore von Breuning.)

The Fischer manuscript:

At the time of the Elector Clemens August, in the year 1724, there lived in the house [Rheingasse 934], the Court Kapellmeister and good singer Maria Joseph Balluinesius [Balduin?] Ludowikus van Beethoven, together with his wife. They had one child, a son, Johann van Beethoven, and lived as tenants on the second floor.

The Court Kapellmeister's son Johann van Beethoven had already received instruction on the piano and in singing at an early age. Later he too was appointed to the post of Court Tenor singer.

Johann van Beethoven also early became an expert in wine-tasting and before long a hearty wine drinker as well; he was light-hearted and merry, being easily satisfied and not intemperate.

When Johann van Beethoven introduced his beloved in person to his father, it was his intention, upon which he insisted and from which he would not waver, that she should become his wife. His father did not consider her as suitable or worthy, although she was a pretty and slender person, with whom no one could find fault, of good law-abiding burgher stock. Moreover, she could prove by means of old references that she had served in good houses where she had received a good upbringing and training.

But after the Court Kapellmeister had obtained information regarding her and had discovered that she had once been a chambermaid, he was very much opposed to the marriage and said to his son, 'I would never have believed or expected of you that you should sink so low.'

19 The Fischer house in Bonn, where the Beethoven family lived from 1776. A Fischer son, Gottfried, wrote a kind of diary which helps to fill in Beethoven's childhood background (engraving by Conrad Caspar Rordorf).

The son of the Court Kapellmeister, Johann van Beethoven, Court Tenor, was married in Bonn in the old parish church of Saint Remigius on 12 November 1767; to Anna Maria Magdelena Keferig, named Beethoven, born in the valley of Ehrenbreitstein. Madame van Beethoven later used to recall that as far as she was concerned she could have had a fine wedding, but that her father-in-law obstinately refused to attend. Because of this the ceremony was brief.

Johann van Beethoven was of medium height, with a long face, broad forehead, a round nose, broad shoulders and serious eyes. He had some scars on his face and wore a thin pigtail. His wife was rather tall, longish face, a nose somewhat bent, spare, earnest eyes. Madame van Beethoven was a clever woman; she could give converse and reply aptly, politely and modestly to high and low, and for this reason she was much liked and respected. She occupied herself with sewing and knitting. They led a righteous and peaceful married life, and paid their house-rent and baker's bills promptly, quarterly and on the day. She was a good domestic woman, she knew how to give and also how to take in manner that is becoming to all people of honest thoughts.

After the Beethovens had had three children, on fine summer days they would be taken out by the serving maids to the Rhine or to the Palace garden, where they played in the sand with other children. At the proper time they would have to find their own way home. When the weather was not favourable, the children played in the Fischers' courtyard with the Fischer and other children from the neighbourhood.

When Johann van Beethoven received visitors and wanted to get rid of the children because they disturbed him, the maid would take them to the lower floor, set them down on the bare floor and control their pranks. The children would then crawl to the entrance door on their hands and knees. As a result of a chill, Nicola [called Johann] suffered an abscess on his head; this resulted in a scar which is still visible.

Beethoven's children were not brought up with gentleness; they were often left in the charge of serving maids. Their father was very strict with them. When the children were with others of their age they could amuse themselves peacefully for a long time. Ludwig liked to be carried piggy-back, which made him laugh heartily.

Johann van Beethoven, the Court Tenor, carried out his duties punctiliously. He gave lessons on the piano and in singing to the sons and daughters of the local English, French and Imperial Envoys, to the gentlemen and daughters of the nobility and to distinguished burghers as well. He often had more to do than he was able, hence his household was well taken care of. The Envoys regarded him with much favour; they had instructed their major-domos that, should he be short of wine, he would send a message and the cellar servants were to bring him full measures of wine to his house. Beethoven, however, availed himself but sparingly of this privilege.   TDR I, 416f., 420f., 423 ff.

Beethoven soon displayed an enormous musical talent, and his father obviously wished to present him as a child prodigy much in the way that Leopold Mozart had capitalized on his son Wolfgang's talents. Johann van Beethoven introduced his son to the world at a concert in Bonn held on 26 March 1778. By this time, Beethoven had begun serious study not only on the organ and piano but also on the violin and viola; he was later to be listed among the viola-players of the Court orchestra. Among his various local teachers the most important, without any question, was Christian Gottlob Neefe (1748–98), who was the Court organist and theatre director at Bonn; from Neefe Beethoven learned Johann Sebastian Bach's *Well-Tempered Clavier*, which he used to play even during his early years in Vienna.

Notice.

On today's date, 26 March 1778, in the hall of the Musical Academy in the Sternengasse, the Court Tenor of the Elector of Cologne BEET-HOVEN will have the honour of presenting two of his pupils, namely Mdelle Averdonc, Court Alto singer, and his young son of six years. The former will have the honour to oblige with several beautiful Arias, the latter with various piano Concerti and Trios. He flatters himself that they will give all the distinguished Ladies and Gentlemen complete

20 Advertisement of Beethoven's first public appearance, 26 March 1778.

21 Christian Gottlob Neefe, Beethoven's first important teacher, was Court organist in Bonn (from a drawing by J. G. Rosenberg).

satisfaction, all the more so since both have had the honour of performing to the greatest satisfaction of the whole Court . . .

TDR I, 120. (Ludwig was in fact seven years old.)

Dr Franz Gerhard Wegeler on Christian Gottlob Neefe:

Neefe had little influence on the education of our Ludwig. The latter
even complained about Neefe's too sharp criticism of his first attempts at
composition.   TDR I, 138.

Beethoven writes to Christian Gottlob Neefe:

Thank you for the counsel you have so often given me in the progress of
my God-given art. Should I ever become a great man, you will have
contributed to it. . . .   Spazier's *Berliner Musikzeitung*, 26 October 1793.

The Fischer manuscript:

When Johann van Beethoven visited the Fischer family of a Sunday
evening, he talked about a number of things. Then he also said: 'My son
Ludwig, he is now my only comfort in life. He is improving in his music
to such an extent that he is admired by everyone. My Ludwig, my
Ludwig, I foresee that in time he will be a great man in the world.
Those of you who are gathered here and see it come about, remember
these words of mine.'

Ludwig van Beethoven, when he was somewhat older, was often
dirty and unkempt, so much so that Cäcilia [Fischer] said to him:
'How dirty you look. You really should be tidier.' To which he answered: 'What difference does it make. When I become a gentleman no
one will notice.'

Once Ludwig van Beethoven was sitting at the window of his bedroom overlooking the courtyard. He held his head in both his hands and
looked very pensive. Cäcilia Fischer, coming across the courtyard,
called up to him: 'What are you looking at, Ludwig?' But she received
no answer. Later she asked him: 'What does that mean? No answer is also
an answer.' He said. 'Oh no, it's not that. Forgive me; I was so taken up
with profound and beautiful thoughts that I could not bear to be disturbed.'

Looking back, one could not say that Ludwig ever cared for companionship or for society. In fact, it was only when he was pondering
over music, or had to occupy himself alone that he would assume quite a
different aspect, and would be conscious of the respect due to him. His
happiest hours were those when he was free of all company, when his
family had all gone out and he could be alone.   TDR I, 442, 427, 436, 434.   31

Beethoven soon began to compose. Unlike Mozart, who was born with a mercurial temperament and a Mendelssohnian facility, Beethoven had to work extremely hard at his compositions, sketching and polishing his works over and over again until he considered them finished; this was a trait of Beethoven's entire career. Since he was a virtuoso on the relatively new piano (in German *Hammerklavier*, generally referred to as Fortepiano), it was natural that many of Beethoven's earliest compositions should be for the piano. His first published works were a set of variations, composed in 1782. His most important compositions of this earliest period, however, were undoubtedly the three piano Sonatas dedicated to the Elector Maximilian Friedrich, WoO 47.

C. F. Cramer's Magazin der Musik *writes about Beethoven, 2 March 1783 :*

Ludwig van Beethoven, son of the above-mentioned Tenor, is an eleven-year-old boy and of very promising talent. He plays on the piano in a very finished manner and powerfully, reads at sight and, to put it briefly, he plays the greater part of the Well Tempered Clavier of Sebastian Bach which Herr Neefe gave him. Those who are familiar with this collection of Preludes and Fugues in every tonality (which one could practically term the *non plus ultra*) will know what this means. Herr Neefe, insofar as his other duties permitted, has given him instruction in thorough–bass. Now he is teaching him composition and in order to encourage him, has had engraved in Mannheim 9 Variations on a March. This young genius deserves a subsidy in order to enable him to travel. He will undoubtedly become a second Mozart, if he progresses as well as he has begun.

Magazin der Musik, year 1, 394. ('The family, and for a long time Ludwig himself, thought he was born in 1772.)

Respectful Pro-Memoria regarding the Electoral Court Musique:

[Bonn, 25 June 1784] . . .

8. Johann Beethoven has a definitely decaying voice; he has been long in service, is very poor, of respectable conduct and married.

13. Christian Neefe, the organist, according to my unprejudiced judgment, could be relieved of this post since he is not particularly accomplished on the organ, is moreover, a foreigner of no particular merit and of the Calvinist religion.

14. Ludwig Beethoven, a son of Beethoven sub no. 8, receives no stipend but, in the absence of Kapellmeister Luchesy, has taken over the organ. He has good ability, is still young and his conduct is quiet and upright. . . .

TDR I, 175 ff.

Cologne Electoral Court and Address Directory for the year 1792:

Tenors.

Messrs. Johann van Beethoven . . .

Organists.

Christian Neefe.

Ludwig van Beethoven . . .

Viola players . . .

Ludwig van Beethoven . . .   Stadtarchiv Bonn.

Anton Schindler writes about Beethoven's youth:

Further or other more outstanding events in any detail regarding Beethoven's life in his native city are not known to us. The long period of peace on the soil of Germany lasted until the beginning of the 1790s. Musicians were bound to their duties at the Courts, at all of which the fostering of music always took pride of place. The concern with earning a livelihood, and also the urge towards further training and the solitude that his budding genius required, the absence of all journalistic publicity and other well-known methods of our present glorious age which transforms our schoolboys into finished artists – it is in these and other internal and external factors that we must seek the reasons why the youth of the composer, who was one day to give his name to an era in German art, is so lacking in significant art-historical incidents. So empty was it of miraculous and romantic anecdotes that the young Beethoven cannot be compared with so many of our youthful prodigy geniuses who, at the same age, . . . astonished the world with operas and symphonies.

Perhaps another reason for this paucity may lie in the fact that our young piano-player, organist and composer endeavoured, from his childhood onward, to be a man in the true meaning of the word and to achieve the most fundamental human principles, in complete antithesis to the musical demi-gods of our own day. And particularly it was his aspiration to achieve his highest task as a man, and from this task he never deviated. This is made clear in a passage from a letter of 29 June 1800 to Wegeler: 'This much I can tell you, that when you see me again I will be really great; not only as an artist but as a man. You will find me better, more fully developed, and if the prosperity of our fatherland has somewhat improved, then shall my art be directed towards the benefit of the poor. Oh happy moment, how fortunate I consider myself that I can contribute to this end, that I myself can bring this to pass!'

Schindler I, 15 f.

22 Fragment of a Violin Concerto in C Major, probably composed by Beethoven in Bonn before the end of 1792.

23 View of Bonn from the Beul side of the Rhine: anonymous coloured etching, probably 1792–94.

It was decided that Beethoven needed more expert guidance than was available in the provincial Court at Bonn, and in 1787 he was sent to Vienna to study with the great Mozart. Beethoven certainly met Mozart in Vienna and heard him play the piano, but it is doubtful whether Ludwig received any serious instruction from Mozart. He had been in Vienna only a few months when he heard that his mother was seriously ill; he broke off his stay in the Austrian capital and returned to Bonn where, in his own words, 'I found my mother still alive but in a wretched state of health' (TDR I, 200). His mother's death was a profound shock, all the more so as Ludwig saw his father Johann becoming a senile alcoholic. Beethoven was now, to all intents and purposes, head of the family and responsible for supporting his two younger brothers, Caspar Anton Carl (1774–1815) and Nikolaus Johann (1776–1848). After he finally moved to Vienna for good in 1792, Beethoven called his brothers there too, and for a time they helped him manage his rather complicated affairs, particularly in dealing with music publishers. Johann became an apothecary and lived in Linz; he later amassed a tidy fortune and bought a small estate at Gneixendorf near Krems on the Danube, where Beethoven visited him in the autumn of 1826. The other brother, who became a banking clerk in Vienna, had a son, Carl, who was later to play an important and extremely unhappy rôle in Beethoven's life. Both brothers married wives of whom Beethoven violently disapproved. Beethoven's father Johann died in December 1792, a month after Beethoven had settled in Vienna.

Dr Gerhard von Breuning describes Beethoven's first visit to Vienna:

Beethoven arrived in Vienna during the winter of 1786–87 and was soon welcomed everywhere with open arms. He found an especially cordial reception from the best-known art-loving families of the aristocracy. Wegeler also soon arrived, in 1787, armed with particularly warm recommendations and subsidies from the Elector. He, like Beethoven, received an entrée into the circle of the celebrated professors and

35

doctors of the Josephinum: Brambilla, Gerhard von Vering, Gottfried van Swieten, Hunczovsky, Adam Schmidt, Wilhelm Schmitt and many others.

Breuning 30.

Carl Czerny writes about Beethoven and Mozart:

In later years Beethoven also told me that he had often heard Mozart play and that, since in his day the invention of the Fortepiano was as yet in its infancy, Mozart had become used to playing in a manner suited to the more customary harpsichords, which was not at all suited to the Forte-piano. Afterwards I made the acquaintance of several people who had studied with Mozart and found that their way of playing fully bore out this observation.

Once, in my house, Beethoven saw the scores of the six Mozart Quartets. He opened the 5th in A [K. 464] and said 'That is a work! In it Mozart said to the world: "See what I could create if the time had come for you!"'

Czerny 14, 11. (Carl Czerny, the inventor of a famous piano method, was, in his youth, a pupil of Beethoven.)

Carl Holz tells Otto Jahn about Beethoven's visit to Mozart:

When he was a boy, Beethoven was taken to Mozart, who told him to play; whereupon he improvised. 'That is very pretty,' said Mozart, 'but

24 Mozart; the famous unfinished oil portrait by J. Lange, *c.* 1790.

25 Ferdinand Ernst Gabriel, Count von Waldstein, as a young man (anonymous).

26 Joseph Haydn; portrait in oils by Thomas Hardy, 1791.

studied.' Beethoven was vexed and asked for a subject on which he improvised in such a way that Mozart said to some friends, 'Watch out for him, he will have something to tell you.'

Kerst II, 185. (Carl Holz, because of his cheerful character, was a very welcome friend of Beethoven's. Otto Jahn, the great biographer of Mozart, also collected material on Beethoven, whose life he intended to write. But he died, in 1869, before he was able to begin his work.)

Beethoven's most important patron in Bonn, apart from the Archbishop and Elector himself, was Ferdinand Ernst Gabriel, Count von Waldstein. He was one of those responsible for persuading the Elector to send Beethoven to Vienna the second time. A trained musician himself, Count Waldstein is said to have encouraged Beethoven in the art of extemporized variations on a given theme, something for which the young composer soon grew famous in Vienna's musical sâlons. As was often the case in relations between Beethoven and his patrons, some frightful quarrel must have occurred between them, for the conversation book of December 1819 quoted below shows that by then they were not even on speaking terms; but Beethoven immortalized their once happy relationship by dedicating to Waldstein one of his very greatest piano Sonatas (Op. 53).

It was now decided that Beethoven should study with Haydn, Mozart having died in December 1791. On his return journey from London in 1792, Haydn was shown a score of Beethoven's *Cantata on the Death of Joseph II*, and immediately accepted Beethoven as a composition pupil. Beethoven arrived in Vienna towards the middle of November 1792 and began to take lessons in counterpoint with Haydn who, however, being extremely busy with compositions for his second London journey, was an inattentive teacher. Nevertheless Haydn recognized that 'Beethoven will in time fill the position of one of Europe's greatest composers and I shall be proud to be able to speak of myself as his teacher . . .'. The rather humorous way Beethoven found to improve his badly corrected counterpoint exercises is detailed in the documents below: Beethoven first went to Johann Baptist Schenk and later, when Haydn returned to England in January 1794, Albrechtsberger took on the job of teaching Beethoven strict counterpoint. Ludwig also studied Italian vocal writing with Antonio Salieri. His first published compositions in Vienna, Op. 1, were three piano Trios, which came out in 1794.

Beethoven was soon famous in Vienna as a pianist and made his début playing the B-Flat Concerto Op. 19 at the Burgtheater on 29 March 1795. The subscription list of the Op. 1 Trios shows that barely two years after he had arrived in Vienna, Beethoven had gained a wide circle of patrons and admirers. Foremost among them was Prince Carl Lichnowsky, a pupil of Mozart's, in whose house Beethoven lived for a time in the mid 1790s; Beethoven dedicated Op. 1 to him, as well as many other important works.

Dedication in Beethoven's album:

Dear Beethowen!

You are now going to Vienna in fulfilment of a wish that has for so long been thwarted. The *genius* of Mozart still mourns and weeps the death of its pupil. It has found a refuge in the inexhaustible Hayden, but no occupation; through him it desires once more to find a union with someone. Through your unceasing diligence, receive Mozart's spirit from the hands of Hayden.

Bonn, the 29th Oct. 792.

Your true friend Waldstein.

Ludwig van Beethovens Stammbuch, facsimile edition with comments by Dr Hans Gerstinger, Bielefeld and Leipzig 1927.

Count Waldstein described by Anton Schindler:

Count Waldstein was a Knight of the German Order, the favourite and the constant companion of the young Elector. Later he became Commander of the German Order in Virnsberg and Chamberlain to the Emperor. He was not only a connoisseur of music but also a practising musician. As such, he was able to exercise a direct influence on the development of Beethoven's young talent. It was on his suggestion that Beethoven developed his ability to conceive and perform variations on an improvised theme, an art in which, during later years, he was unrivalled, let alone excelled, by any of his contemporaries. . . . To what extent Count von Waldstein already valued Beethoven's talent immediately following these first indications, and what a future he predicted for him, is apparent from a letter he wrote to the young composer, the contents of which are given [above, previous document]. From Wegeler,

moreover, we learn that this true nobleman provided the young composer with several financial subsidies which, in order to spare Beethoven's sensitivity, were generally passed off as a small munificence from the Elector. It should also be recalled that Beethoven, when at the peak of his artistic career, openly expressed his gratitude to this patron, protector and fellow artist, by the dedication of his great Sonata in C Major, Op. 53, which was published in 1806.
Schindler I, 6.

Letter from Joseph Haydn to Maximilian Franz, Elector of Cologne:
Serene Electoral Highness!

I humbly take the liberty of sending Your Serene Electoral Highness some musical works, viz. a Quintet, an eight-part Parthie, an oboe Concerto, Variations for the Fortepiano, and a Fugue, compositions of my dear pupil Beethoven, with whose care I have been graciously entrusted. I flatter myself that these pieces, which I may recommend as evidence of his assiduity over and above his actual studies, may be graciously accepted by Your Serene Electoral Highness. Connoisseurs and non-connoisseurs must candidly admit, from these present pieces, that Beethoven will in time fill the position of one of Europe's greatest composers, and I shall be proud to be able to speak of myself as his teacher, I only wish that he might remain with me a little while longer.

While we are on the subject of Beethoven, Your Serene Electoral Highness will perhaps permit me to say a few words concerning his financial status. 100 [Ducats] were allotted to him during the past year. Your Serene Electoral Highness is no doubt convinced that this sum was insufficient, and not even enough to live on; undoubtedly Your Highness also had his own reasons for choosing to send him into the great world with such a paltry sum. Under these circumstances and to prevent him from falling into the hands of usurers, I have in part gone bail for him and in part lent him money myself, with the result that he owes me 500 fl., of which not a Kreutzer was spent unnecessarily; which sum I would ask you to send to him here. And since the interest on borrowed money grows continually and is in any case very tedious for an artist like Beethoven, I think that if Your Serene Electoral Highness were to send him 1000 fl. for the coming year, Your Highness would earn his eternal gratitude, and at the same time relieve him of all his distress. For the teachers who are absolutely essential for him, and the display which is necessary if he is to gain admission into numerous salons, reduce this sum to such an extent that only the bare minimum remains. As for the extravagance which one fears will tempt any young man who goes into the great world, I think I can answer for that to Your Serene Electoral Highness; for a hundred circumstances have confirmed me in my opinion that he is capable of sacrificing everything without any restraint for his art. In view of so many tempting occasions, this is most remarkable, and gives every security to Your Serene Electoral Highness – in view of the gracious kindness that we expect – that your Highness will not be wasting any of your grace on usurers as far as Beethoven is concerned. In the hope that Your Serene Electoral Highness will continue his further patronage of my dear pupil by graciously acceding to this my request, I am, with profound respect,

Your Serene Electoral Highness'
most humble and obedient
Joseph Haydn.
Kapellmeister of Prince Nicolaus Esterházy.

Vienna, 23 November 1793.

The Collected Correspondence and London Notebooks of Joseph Haydn, ed. H.C. Robbins Landon, London 1959, 141 f.

Jahrbuch der Tonkunst von Wien und Prag, 1796, writes about Beethoven and Albrechtsberger:

Beethoven, a musical genius, has chosen Vienna as his residence for the past two years. He is widely admired for the unusual velocity of his playing, and is astounding in the way he masters the most formidable difficulties with the greatest of ease. He seems already to have entered into the inner sanctuary of music, distinguishing himself for his precision, feeling and taste; consequently his fame has risen considerably. A living proof of his true love of art lies in the fact that he has put himself in the hands of our immortal Haydn in order to be initiated into the holy secrets of the art of music. The latter great Master, during his absence, has turned him over to our great Albrechtsberger. What cannot be expected when such a great genius places himself under the guidance of such excellent masters! There have already been several beautiful Sonatas by him, among which his latest [Op. 2] is regarded as particularly outstanding.

Kerst I, 30.

Letter from Albrechtsberger to Beethoven (15 December 1796):

My very best wishes for your name-day tomorrow. May God give you health and satisfaction and grant you much good fortune. My dear

27 Johann Baptist Schenk, who taught Beethoven after Haydn (anonymous).

28 Johann Georg Albrechtsberger, Beethoven's teacher in counterpoint (anonymous).

Beethoven, if you should happen to have an hour at your disposal, your old teacher invites you to spend it with him.

Stephen Ley, *Wahrheit, Zweifel und Irrtum in der Kunde von Beethovens Leben* Wiesbaden 1955, p. 7.

Dolezalek to Jahn, 30 October 1852:

At that time, composers were inimical towards Beethoven, whom they did not understand and who had a sharp tongue. Dolezalek brought an article* about a quartet by Beethoven.
Albrechtsberger: 'Who is that thing by?'
Dolezalek: 'Beethoven.'
Albrechtsberger: 'Ah, don't have anything to do with him. He has learned nothing and will never amount to anything.'
Kotzeluch threw the C minor trio on the floor when he [Dolezalek] played it to him.

Kerst II, 191. (Johann Nepomuk Emanuel Dolezalek, a good musician, knew Beethoven when he was a young man and related his reminiscences of Beethoven to Otto Jahn on 30 October 1852. Kotzeluch was a popular but mediocre composer.)

Johann Schenk about his pupil Beethoven:

In 1792, His Imperial Highness, Archduke Maximilian, Elector of Cologne, was pleased to send his protégé Louis van Beethoven to Vienna

* German *Arbeit*, which means literally 'work', i.e. either an article about the quartet or, perhaps, a *Bearbeitung* (arrangement) which Dolezalek made.

in order that he might study musical composition with Joseph Haydn. Towards the end of July [1793] the Abbé Gelinek informed me that he had made the acquaintance of a young man who displayed a rare virtuosity on the pianoforte, such as he had not heard since Mozart. At the same time he explained that Beethoven had begun to study counterpoint with Haydn more than six months before, but was still at work on the first exercise. He also said that His Excellency Baron van Swieten had warmly recommended the study of counterpoint to him and often inquired how far he had progressed in his studies. On Beethoven's writing desk I came across a few phrases of the first exercise in counterpoint. After a cursory examination it was clear to me that in every tonality (short as these were) there were several mistakes. This tended to bear out the truth of Gelinek's above-mentioned remarks. Since I was now convinced that my pupil was ignorant of the primary rules of counterpoint, I gave him the universally known text-book by Joseph Fux, *Gradus ad Parnassum*, so that he might obtain a summary of the subsequent exercises. Joseph Haydn, who had returned to Vienna from London towards the end of the previous year, was engaged in harnessing his Muse to the composition of great new masterpieces. Taken up with these important endeavours, it was clear that Haydn could not easily occupy himself with teaching grammar. Now I was seriously anxious to be of assistance to one so eager to acquire knowledge. Before I began to teach him, however, I pointed out to him that our work together must forever remain a secret. In this regard, I ordered him to copy out once again every passage which I had corrected in my own hand, so that every time Haydn examined it he would not notice the work of a strange hand. A year later, Beethoven came into conflict with Gelinek, the cause of which I have forgotten. It seems to me, however, that both sides were to blame. As a result of their dispute, Gelinek became angry and revealed my secret. Beethoven and his brothers made no secret of it. . . .

In about mid-May [1793] he informed me that he would shortly go to Eisenstadt with Haydn and would stay there until the beginning of winter. He did not yet know the day of departure. At the beginning of June I went to his house at the usual hour – but my good Louis was nowhere to be seen. He had left me the following little note which I transcribe word for word.

'Dear Schenk,

'I wish that I did not have to depart today for Eisenstadt. I would have liked to talk with you once more. In the meanwhile, you may count on my gratitude for the kindnesses you have shown me. I will make every effort to return them. I hope to see you again soon and to enjoy the pleasure of your company. Farewell and do not entirely forget

your
Beethoven.'

TDR I, 329 ff. (Schenk wrote this document in summer 1830.)

Schindler describes Beethoven's meeting with Schenk:

One day in the spring of 1824, Beethoven was walking along the Graben with me, when we met Schenk. Beethoven was beside himself with joy at seeing once more this old friend of whom he had not heard for many years; he seized his hand and dragged him off to the nearby inn called *Zum Jägerhorn* and into the back room which had to be lit up even in the daytime. In order to remain undisturbed he closed the door. Then he began to open up all the secrets of his heart. After complaints about bad luck and description and discussion of misfortunes, events of the years 1793–94 were recalled. Upon which Beethoven broke out into loud laughter, remembering how they both had played a trick on father Haydn, who had never noticed anything. This scene was the occasion of my hearing for the first time about the unusual relationship which had existed between the two men. Beethoven, who at that moment stood at the summit of his art, overwhelmed the modest composer of the *Dorfbarbier* as well as the grand opera *Achmet und Almanzine* and several other *Singspiele*, and who lived by giving lessons, with the most fervent gratitude for the part he had played during his years of study and for his friendly devotion. The leave-taking of the two after that remarkable hour was moving, as if it were for life, and indeed so it was – Beethoven and Schenk never saw one another again after that day.
Schindler I, 31 f.

From Ignaz Moscheles' diary:

[1808] How astonished I was one day when I saw at the home of Court Kapellmeister Salieri, whom I had not found at home, a note written in capital letters lying on the table which read 'The pupil Beethoven was here'. That made me think. A Beethoven can still learn something from a Salieri? How much more could I! Salieri had been the pupil and the warmest admirer of Gluck. Only he refused to recognize the value of Mozart and his works; that was well known. And yet I went to him, became his pupil, and was, for three years, his assistant at the Opera. On account of this, I received permission to visit every theatre without payment. It was a light-hearted and very stirring existence in my beloved Vienna.

Aus Ignaz Moscheles Leben, ed. by his wife, Leipzig 1872, p. 11. (Ignaz Moscheles, born in 1794, was the most famous pianist of his day.)

Carl Czerny describes Beethoven's piano-playing:

Mozart's school: clear and markedly brilliant playing based more on staccato than legato; a witty and lively execution. The pedal is rarely used and never necessary.

Beethoven's manner: characteristic and passionate strength, alternating with all the charms of a smooth *cantabile*, is its outstanding feature. . . .

Beethoven, who appeared around 1790, drew entirely new and daring passages from the Fortepiano by the use of the pedal, by an exceptionally characteristic way of playing, particularly distinguished by a strict legato of the chords, and thus created a new type of singing tone and many hitherto unimagined effects. His playing did not possess that clean and brilliant elegance of certain other pianists. On the other hand, it was spirited, grandiose and, especially in adagio, very full of feeling and romantic. His performance, like his compositions, was a tone-painting of a very high order and conceived only for a total effect.

Carl Czerny, *Vollständige theoretisch-praktische Pianoforte Schule*, Vienna n.d. Part III, Ch. 15. Kerst I, 63.

Wiener Zeitung *of 1 April 1795:*

On 29 and 30 March, in the Imperial Royal Court Theatre near the Burg, an oratorio devised by Herr Kapellmeister Kartellieri, entitled *Joas, King of Judah,*★ was performed at the regular large concert of the local *Tonkünstler-Gesellschaft* [Society of Musical Artists] for the benefit of the widows' and orphans' fund. . . . . As an intermezzo, on the first evening, the celebrated Herr Ludwig van Beethoven reaped the unanimous applause of the audience for his performance on the pianoforte of a completely new concerto [in B-Flat, Op. 19] composed by him.

Ferdinand Ries describes Beethoven's relations with Haydn:

The three Trios by Beethoven (Op. 1) were to be performed for the first time before the art world at a soirée given by Prince Lichnowsky. The majority of artists and music-lovers had been invited, in particular

★ Correctly: *Gioas, re di Giuda* by Casimir Antonio Cartellieri (1772–1807).

Haydn, whose verdict everybody was most eager to hear. The Trios were played and immediately aroused great interest. Haydn, too, said many good things about them but advised Beethoven not to publish the third Trio in C Minor. This surprised Beethoven very much, inasmuch as he considered it the best, just as today it is still the most popular and arouses the greatest enthusiasm. Because of this, Haydn's remark made a bad impression on Beethoven and led him to believe that Haydn was envious, jealous and badly disposed towards him. I must admit that when Beethoven said this to me, I did not really believe it. I then took the opportunity of asking Haydn himself. His answer, however, confirmed Beethoven's remarks, inasmuch as he said that he had not believed this Trio would have been so quickly and easily understood and so favourably received by the public.

WRBN 84 f. (Ferdinand Ries had been Beethoven's pupil.)

29 Autograph page of Beethoven's Rondo for Pianoforte with Orchestra, which seems to have served originally as the finale to the Piano Concerto in B-Flat, Op. 19.

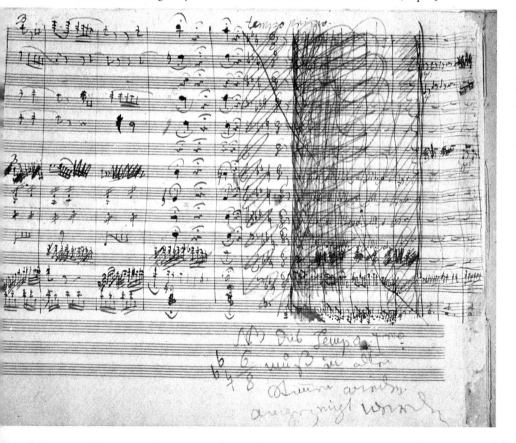

Anton Schindler about Beethoven's relations with Haydn:

It is permissible, however, to be surprised by Haydn's opinion when one is acquainted with his own Trios. As far as I am concerned I place the event in the long series of misunderstandings of which there were, unfortunately, too many in Beethoven's life.

Schindler I, 54.

Frau von Bernhard writes about Beethoven and Prince Lichnowsky:

When he [Beethoven] came to us, he used to stick his head in the door and make sure that there was no one there whom he disliked. He was small and plain-looking with an ugly red, pock-marked face. His hair was quite dark and hung almost shaggily around his face. His clothes were very commonplace, not differing greatly from the fashion of those days, particularly in our circles. Moreover, he spoke in a strong dialect and in a rather common manner. In general his whole being did not give the impression of any particular cultivation; in fact, he was un-mannerly in both gesture and demeanour. He was very haughty; I myself have seen the mother of Princess Lichnowsky, Countess Thun, going down on her knees to him as he lolled on the sofa, and begging him to play something. But Beethoven did not. Countess Thun was, however, a very eccentric woman.

I was frequently invited to the Lichnowskys, in order to play there. He was a friendly and distinguished gentleman and she a very beautiful woman. Yet they did not seem happy together; she always had such a melancholy expression on her face, and I heard that he spent a great deal of money, far beyond his means. Her sister [Elisabeth, married to Count Razumovsky], who was even more beautiful, had a husband who was a patron of Beethoven. She was almost always present when music was performed. I still remember clearly both Haydn and Salieri sitting on a sofa on one side of the small music-room, both carefully dressed in the old-fashioned way with perruque, shoes and silk hose, whereas even here Beethoven would come dressed in the informal fashion of the other side of the Rhine, almost ill-dressed.

Kerst I, 24. (Frau von Bernhard came to Vienna as a young girl to complete her training as a pianist.)

Carl Czerny writes about Prince Lichnowsky:

In 1804 I was presented by Krumpholz to Prince Lichnowsky, Beethoven's friend and most active supporter. The prince, as well as his brother, Count Moritz, had previously both been pupils of Mozart and later of Beet-

30 Carl Prince Lichnowsky; anonymous oil portrait. Beethoven lived for a time in the same house as Lichnowsky, who was a great admirer of the composer.

31 Marie Christiane Princess Lichnowsky, *née* Countess Thun; anonymous oil portrait. Like her husband, the Princess had been a pupil of Mozart.

hoven; they were great connoisseurs of the arts as well as the most amiable and humane of men. It was Prince Lichnowsky who had brought the young Beethoven to Vienna and enabled him to study with Haydn, Salieri and Albrechtsberger. He treated him like a friend and brother and persuaded the whole of the high nobility to support him.

Czerny 11. (Wenzel Krumpholz [1750–1817] was a violinist at the Court Opera, Vienna, and also a composer. Beethoven was very fond of him.)

Dr Franz Wegeler and Ferdinand Ries describe Beethoven's character:

Beethoven, who had been brought up under straitened circumstances and at the same time under guardianship, though merely that of his friends, had no idea about the value of money and was anything but economical. To give an example: dinner-time at Prince Carl Lichnowsky's was set for four o'clock. 'Now I'm supposed to be home every day at half-past three,' said Beethoven, 'shave, change into something better, etc. I could never endure that.' So it happened that he often went to inns, where he came off badly, as in all matters of economy, since he did not, as stated above, have any understanding of the value of things or of money. The Prince, who had a very loud metallic voice, once gave an order to his valet, in the event that he and Beethoven rang at the same time, to attend the latter first. Beethoven overheard this and on the same day engaged a servant of his own. In the same way, the Prince made available to him a mount from his well-filled stable. Beethoven thereupon procured a horse of his own when he was taken with the notion, but soon abandoned the idea of learning to ride. . . . This Andante of the *Waldstein Sonata* has left me with a sad memory. When Beethoven played it to Krumpholz (whose death in 1817 upset Beethoven greatly) and myself for the first time, it gave us the utmost pleasure and we tormented him unceasingly until he repeated it. On my way home, passing by the house of Prince Lichnowsky, I went in to tell him about Beethoven's wonderful new composition and was obliged to play him the piece as well as I could remember it. As I remembered more and more of it, the Prince requested me to repeat it once more. So it came about that even the Prince learned a part of it. In order to surprise Beethoven, the Prince went to him the next day and told him that he, too, had composed something which was not at all bad. Beethoven's firm declaration that he did not wish to hear it went unheeded; the Prince sat down and played, to Beethoven's astonishment, a good part of the Andante.

Beethoven was very annoyed about this, and it was because of that occasion that I never heard Beethoven play again. For he would never again play in my presence and several times insisted that I should leave the room when he played. One day, when a small party, which included both Beethoven and myself, breakfasted with the Prince after the concert in the Augarten (at eight o'clock in the morning). it was suggested that we should go to Beethoven's house in order to hear his as yet unfinished opera, *Leonore*. When we arrived there Beethoven requested, even this time, that I should go away. Since the insistent requests of all those present were fruitless, I left with tears in my eyes. The whole company noticed it. Prince Lichnowsky, coming after me, asked that I be allowed to wait in the anteroom; since he had been to blame for the whole occasion he now wished it to be settled. My offended sense of honour would not allow it. I heard afterwards that Lichnowsky was very violent with Beethoven on account of his behaviour, for it was only his love of Beethoven's works which had occasioned the whole affair as well as Beethoven's resulting anger. But the only outcome of these remonstrances was that henceforth he never again played at private parties.

WRBN 33, 102 f.

32 The publishing house of Artaria & Co. on the Kohlmarkt in Vienna; engraving by Wett, drawn and coloured by A. Leithner.

Beethoven's début as an orchestral composer in Vienna took place on Sunday, 22 November 1795, St Cecilia's Day. Beethoven conducted Twelve Minuets (WoO 7) and Twelve German Dances (WoO 8) for the famous ball of the pension fund of the Society of Artists, for which Haydn and Mozart had composed most of their greatest dance music for orchestra. These masked balls were held at the Redoutensaal on the Josephsplatz in Vienna and usually, each year, two composers were asked to write the dances, one for the large room and one for the small room. Haydn had composed the Minuets and German Dances for the 1792 season and was probably responsible for getting Beethoven the commission in 1795. When Haydn returned from London in the late summer of 1795, he and Beethoven often appeared together at concerts, Haydn conducting and Beethoven playing the piano. Haydn launched three of his new Salomon Symphonies, composed in 1794 and 1795, at a concert in the Redoutensaal on 16 December 1795, and Beethoven played his Piano Concerto Op. 19. A few weeks later, on 8 January 1796, they again collaborated at such a concert in the Redoutensaal, this time for the benefit of the singer Maria Bolla. Beethoven was now becoming not only a successful pianist but a highly successful composer. Among the many Viennese publishers who clamoured to print his latest works was the distinguished firm of Artaria & Co. on the Kohlmarkt; Artaria had published many of Haydn's and Mozart's compositions and they immediately issued, for instance, the successful Minuets and German Dances that Beethoven had composed for the Redoutensaal.

33 The Redoutensaal in the Hofburg, Vienna; engraving by J. Schütz, *c.* 1800. Beethoven was commissioned to provide orchestral music for a charity ball here in 1795.

Wiener Zeitung *of 14 November 1795, No. 91:*

The masked ball for the Pension Fund of the Society of Artists will be given this year on Sunday, 22 November, in the Imperial-Royal Ballroom. The music for the Minuets and German Dances for this ball will once again be in new arrangements. For the small ballroom the music has been composed by the master hand of Herr Ludwig van Beethoven as a token of his desire for solidarity between the various branches of the arts.

Wiener Zeitung *of 16 December 1795, No. 100:*

Musical Academy.

   On Friday next, the 18th inst., Herr Kapellmeister Haydn will give a large musical academy in the small Ballroom, in which Mad. Tomeoni und Herr Mombelli will sing; Herr van Beethoven will play a concerto of his own composition on the Fortepiano; and three symphonies, not previously heard here, which Herr Kapellmeister [Haydn] composed during his last visit to London, will be performed. Admission tickets may be obtained from Herr Kapellmeister Haydn at his residence on the Neuen Markt, in the Hoföbstlerisches Haus, third floor, at all hours.

Beethoven now had a very wide circle of friends and colleagues. Among them was the famous actor Johann Heinrich Friedrich Müller, who lived in a big apartment-house complex called the Bürgerspital, next to the Kärntnerthortheater, one of Vienna's two principal theatres (the other was the Burgtheater, where Mozart had first conducted *Figaro* and Haydn was to conduct the first public performance of *The Creation* in 1798). In the Bürgerspital there also lived a Hungarian aristocrat, Nikolaus Zmeskall von Domanowecz, an excellent cellist who often participated in quartet parties and chamber music. He remained one of Beethoven's most faithful friends and the composer dedicated his Quartet in F minor, Op. 95, to him. Later Zmeskall grew old and infirm, but it is touching to think that he was taken in a sedan chair to hear the first performance of the Ninth Symphony in 1824.

Letter from Beethoven on 16 December 1816 to Zmeskall:

Here, my dear Z, receive my affectionate dedication which I hope you will accept as a loving memento of our long friendship, and as a token of my esteem, and not consider it the end of what is now a long drawn-out thread (for you are one among my oldest friends in Vienna). . . .
KHV 268. (The dedication was the Quartet Op. 95.)

Ferdinand Ries describes Beethoven's stubbornness:

Haydn had wished Beethoven to put 'Pupil of Haydn' on the title-page of his first work. Beethoven did not want to do this because he had, as he

34 The Kärntnerthortheater, Vienna, *c.* 1825 (anonymous engraving).

said, taken some lessons from Haydn but had never learned anything from him. (During his first visit to Vienna he had received some instruction from Mozart but the latter had, as Beethoven complained, never played to him.) Beethoven had also studied counterpoint with Albrechtsberger and dramatic music with Salieri. I knew them all well; all three thought highly of Beethoven, but they all were of one mind regarding his learning. Each one of them said that Beethoven was always so stubborn and self-willed that he had to learn from his own bitter experience what he had never been willing to accept in the course of his lessons. Particularly Albrechtsberger and Salieri were of this opinion: the dry rules of the former and the insignificant ones of the latter in dramatic composition (following the old Italian school) meant nothing to Beethoven.   WRBN 86.

Early in 1796, Beethoven went on a journey to Prague in the company of Prince Lichnowsky (Mozart and Lichnowsky had made a similar trip some years before). This first big concert tour of Beethoven's was an enormous success, and after a brief return to Vienna he set out for Leipzig, Dresden and Berlin, where he gave concerts. In Prague, he composed the beautiful *scena* 'Ah, perfido!' for Josephine, Countess von Clary, who later married the famous musical patron of Prague, Christian Count Clam-Gallas. 'Ah, perfido!' (Op. 65), closely modelled on Haydn's *Scena di Berenice* (1795), was soon taken into the repertoire of Madame Josepha Duschek, one of Mozart's friends and a brilliant dramatic soprano. In Berlin, Beethoven met the well-known pianist Friedrich Heinrich Himmel and played to Friedrich Wilhelm II, King of Prussia. There Beethoven composed the Cello Sonatas Op. 5 for Jean

35 Nikolaus Zmeskall von Domanowecz, Hungarian diplomat and cellist, who became an intimate friend of Beethoven's (anonymous silhouette).

36 Antonio Salieri, Mozart's great rival, taught Beethoven operatic and vocal composition (anonymous oil portrait).

37 Josephine Countess von Clary was a well-known amateur singer for whom Beethoven wrote 'Ah perfido!' (miniature on ivory by C.J.A. Agricola).

Louis Duport, a famous virtuoso cellist in the service of the King. In November 1796, we find Beethoven giving a concert in the handsome coronation city of Pressburg (now Bratislava, CSSR) and writing home to his friend, the piano manufacturer Johann Andreas Streicher, about the concert and about the piano. The Fortepiano was now developing very quickly, its keyboard was being extended in both treble and bass, and an attempt was being made to increase its resonance and sonority. Beethoven, when he first came to Vienna, used to play on pianos made by Anton Walter, then the leading piano manufacturer, who had also supplied Mozart's beautiful instrument (now in the Mozarteum in Salzburg) as well as instruments for Eszterháza Castle (one is now in the Haydn Museum in Eisenstadt).

Letter from Beethoven to his brother Nikolaus Johann:

Prague, 19 February [1796]

Dear Brother,

I must write to you so that you will at least know where I am and what I am doing. In the first place, things are going well with me, very well indeed. My art wins me friends and renown. What more can I want? And this time I will earn quite a lot of money. I shall remain here for another few weeks, and then go to Dresden, Leipzig and Berlin. It will be surely at least six weeks before I return. I hope that you will enjoy your stay in Vienna more and more. But have a care for the whole tribe of bad women. Have you already been to see cousin Elss [?]. You can write to me here once more, if you want to and have the time.

P[rince] Lichnowsky will soon return to Vienna. He has already departed from here. In case you should need money, you may make bold and go to him, for he still owes me. And now, I hope that your life may be ever happier, and I would like to contribute something to it. Farewell, my dear brother, and think sometimes of your true and faithful brother,

L. Beethoven.

Greet brother Caspar [heavily crossed out, but later underlined].

My address is: Im goldenen Einhorn auf der Kleinseite

Address: To be delivered to my brother Nicolaus Beethoven care of the Apothecary by the Kärnthner Thor.

Herr von Z[meskall] will be so kind as to give this letter to the wig-maker who will forward it.

KAL 19f. (Cousin Elss may very well be related to Emmerich Joseph Philipp Johann Nepomuk Count Eltz [*recte*], at that time Envoy at the Court of Saxony, to whom Beethoven brought some letters in Dresden.)

Letter from August von Schall to the Elector Maximilian Franz:

[Dresden, 6 May 1796]

Beethoven was here for about eight days. Everyone who heard him play on the clavier was delighted. With the Elector of Saxony, who is a connoisseur of music, Beethoven had the privilege of playing accompaniments for one and a half hours. His Electoral Highness was exception-ally satisfied and presented him with a gold snuff-box. Beethoven has left Dresden for Leipzig and Berlin. He expressly requested me, when I had time and opportunity, to lay his homage most respectfully at your Serene Electoral Highness's feet and to beg for your Gracious further favour. . . .

Hans Volkmann: *Beethoven in seinen Beziehungen zu Dresden*, Dresden 1942, p. 24. (August von Schall was the Marshal of the Court of the Elector Maximilian Franz. He had already shown much interest in Beethoven in Bonn and recommended him to his cousin in Dresden, the Envoy of the Elector Palatine, Count Carl Theodor von Schall, so that he might smooth his path in Dresden.)

Johann Friedrich Reichardt on Streicher's pianos, 7 February 1809:

Streicher has abandoned the softness of the other Viennese instruments, with their too delicate touch and bouncing rolling action, and on Beethoven's advice and request has given his instruments a more resisting touch and elastic action, so that the virtuoso who executes with strength and meaning has more control of his instrument in sustaining and carry-ing, in the striking and releasing [of the keys]. He thereby gives his instruments a stronger and more varied character, so that they should satisfy every virtuoso, who doesn't seek merely a light brilliance in his playing, more than any other instrument. . . .   Reichardt I, 311.

Letter from Beethoven to Johann Andreas Streicher, about 1796:

Most excellent Streicher!

I really must beg your pardon for being so late in answering your very obliging letter. If I tell you that I was prevented from doing so by the pressure of my almost overwhelming work, I assure you that I am not telling you a lie. Your little pupil, my dear St., apart from drawing a couple of tears from my eyes by her playing of my Adagio, has aroused my admiration. I wish you every good luck; you are fortunate in being able to display your understanding through the medium of such talent. And I am happy that this dear talented child has you for a master. Honestly, I assure you that this is the first time I have felt pleasure in hearing my Trio. Truly this will decide me to write more for the piano than heretofore. Even if only a few people understand me I will be satisfied. Undoubtedly, the manner of playing the piano is as yet the least developed form of instrumental playing. One often imagines one is listening to a harp, and I am happy, my dear friend, that you are one of the few who realize and feel that one can also sing on the piano, so long as one has feeling. I hope that the time will come when the harp and the piano will be regarded as two completely different instruments. For that matter, I think you may allow the girl to play everywhere. Between ourselves, she will put certain of our commonplace and conceited hurdy-gurdy grinders to shame.

One more thing: Would you take it amiss, my very good St., if I too have a small share in her training? That is, if I take an interest in her progress. For, while not wanting to flatter you, I cannot think of anything better to tell her than that you should oversee her and her progress, and encourage her on my behalf. Now, farewell, my dear St., and continue to be my friend, as I am entirely

your true friend,
L. v. Beethoven.

I hope to be able to visit you soon; then I will give you the number of my lodgings. Give my greetings to your dear wife.

Sonneck 183. Anderson 18.

One of Beethoven's colleagues was Ignaz Schuppanzigh, an excellent violinist who was to play the first performances of all Beethoven's string quartets and many of his other pieces of chamber music. Beethoven's circle of patrons was also growing rapidly. Among them was Johann Joseph, Prince von Schwarzenberg, at whose winter palace on the Mehlmarkt Haydn's *Creation* was first performed in 1798 and where Beethoven's very popular Septet Op. 20 was first heard. Another excellent patron was Johann Joseph, Prince von Liechtenstein, whose beautiful wife (née

Landgravine Fürstenberg) was a pupil of Beethoven's, and to whom Beethoven dedicated the lovely Piano Sonata Op. 27, No. 1. Still another interesting patron and pupil of Beethoven's was Anna Luisa Barbara (Babette), Princess Odescalchi, née Countess von Keglevics de Buzin, to whom Beethoven dedicated, among other things, his Piano Concerto in C, Op. 15. He gave concerts at the Odescalchis', including a performance of the Septet, about which he writes to Zmeskall. The year that Haydn finished his *Creation*, 1798, saw the publication of Beethoven's *Sonate pathétique*, Op. 13, a landmark in Beethoven's *œuvre* and in the history of the piano as well. In the seven years since Mozart's death, the piano had already been enlarged considerably, and if it was by no means the powerful instrument of Beethoven's maturity, it was nonetheless capable of dynamic gradations not hitherto found in anything except Haydn's late London sonatas (a group of composers and pianists in London, such as Muzio Clementi and J. B. Cramer, were enlarging the piano's range and scope quite independently of the Viennese school).

Carl Czerny describes the violinist Schuppanzigh:

Among Beethoven's friends Schuppanzigh was exceptionally note-worthy.

One would not have imagined, when seeing this short, fat, pleasure-loving young man (whom Beethoven only referred to as his Falstaff), that he should be possessed of so fine and ingenious a spirit. As one of the best violin-players of that time, he was unrivalled in quartet playing, a very good concert artist and the best orchestra conductor of his day.

Since he himself was not a composer, he was not swayed by any form of egotism from following Beethoven with unshakable faithfulness, and using every aspect of his performing ability to ensure that Beethoven's works might be presented to the public in all their greatness and beauty. Moreover, no one knew how to enter into the spirit of this music better than he: in fact, such a friend was of the greatest usefulness to Beethoven. Czerny 12.

Johann Friedrich Reichardt writes about the Schuppanzigh Quartet:

Vienna, 10 December 1808.
Today I must tell you about the very fine quartet of Herr Schuppanzigh, a good violinist, which has opened a subscription series for the winter under the patronage of Count von Razumovsky, the former Russian Envoy at the Imperial Court in Vienna. Performances will take place every Thursday from twelve to two in a private house. Last Thursday we heard it for the first time. Actually, there was not a large assembly there, but one consisting of very zealous and attentive music-lovers. And that is the proper public for this finest and most intimate of all musical associations.

38 Ignaz Schuppanzigh, one of Beethoven's close friends, was an excellent solo violinist who also liked to direct orchestral performances (lithograph by B. E. von Schrötter).

39 Autograph page of the String Quartet in C, Op. 59 No. 3, one of three which Beethoven composed in 1805–06 and dedicated to Count Razumovsky.

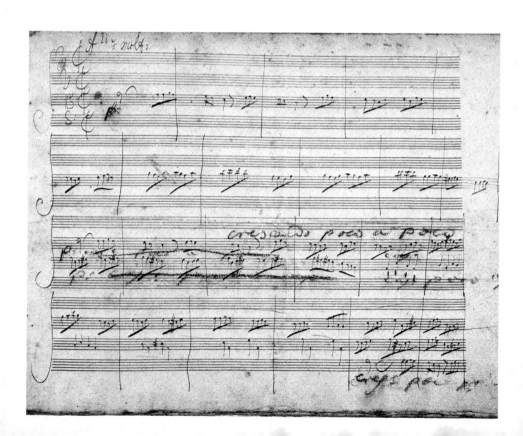

40 Andreas Cyrillovich Prince Razumovsky; miniature on paper by J. Le Gros, 1820. The immensely wealthy Prince was Russian ambassador to the Austrian Court. In 1808, he founded a string quartet in which he himself occasionally played second violin. He placed this quartet at Beethoven's disposal for performances of his chamber music.

This quartet was on the whole very well put together, although some people claim that last year, together with Herr Kraft, this was even more the case. Herr Schuppanzigh has an individual piquant way of playing which is very suitable to the humorous quartets of Haydn, Mozart and Beethoven; or perhaps, rather, it resulted from a measured whimsical reading of those masterpieces. He executes with clarity, though not always absolutely cleanly, the most difficult passages, which the local virtuosi seem to avoid altogether. He also accents very correctly and significantly. His *cantabile* is often truly singing and moving. He also leads his well-picked colleagues skilfully and truly in the spirit of the composer; but he often disturbs me on account of the damnable habit, which has crept into use here, of beating time with his foot, even when it is not necessary, often out of sheer habit and often only to reinforce a *forte*. In general one rarely hears a *forte* here, or even a *fortissimo*, without the leader's pounding violently with his foot.

Reichardt I, 162, 164.

Dolezalek on Beethoven's Septet:

The Septet was first performed at Prince Schwarzenberg's and was much admired. 'That is my Creation' [said Beethoven, with reference to Haydn's oratorio *The Creation*, which had also been performed for the first time in the Schwarzenberg palace].

Kerst II, 192.

41 Joseph Johann Prince von Schwarzenberg had his own orchestra and performed several works of Beethoven in his various palaces and castles (anonymous copy of a painting by A. F. Oelenhainz).

42 The Schwarzenberg Palace on the Mehlmarkt, Vienna, *c.* 1825 (anonymous engraving).

Dr Franz Wegeler writes about Beethoven's dislike of playing in society:

Later, when Beethoven had already achieved a high position in Vienna, he expressed a similar, if not even more violent, aversion to being asked to play at social gatherings; every time this happened he would lose all his cheerfulness. On several occasions he came to me in a gloomy and ill-humoured mood, complaining that people forced him to play even if the blood was burning under his fingernails. Gradually a conversation would develop between us, in the course of which I would try to calm him down. When my aim had been satisfactorily achieved, I would let the conversation drop and sit down at my desk, and Beethoven, if he wanted to go on talking to me, would be obliged to sit on the chair in front of the piano. With an uncertain hand, and often still turned around, he would pick out a few chords from which, little by little, would develop the most beautiful melodies. Alas, why did I not understand more about it! Once, in order to obtain some manuscript from him, I had, to all intents and purposes accidentally, left music paper on the stand. He wrote on it, but in the end it was folded and placed in his pocket! All that was left to me was the permission to laugh at myself.

About his playing I could say nothing, or only very little, and that, as it were, in passing. He would then leave quite relaxed and would always come back again with pleasure. Nevertheless, this aversion remained with him and was often the source of the bitterest quarrels with his best friends and patrons.

WRBN 19f.

Ferdinand Ries on Beethoven and the Princess Liechtenstein:

One evening I was due to play at Count Browne's a Sonata by Beethoven (A Minor, Op. 23), a work not often heard. Since Beethoven was present and since I had not practised this Sonata with him, I declared that I was ready to play any other Sonata but not that one. People turned to Beethoven, who finally said, 'Surely you will not play it so badly that I will not be able to listen to it.' So I was obliged to play it. As usual, Beethoven turned pages for me. In a jump in the left hand, where one particular note must be brought out, I went completely astray and Beethoven tapped me on the head with one finger. Princess L[iechtenstein], who sat leaning on the piano facing me, watched this with amusement. When I had finished playing, Beethoven said, 'Very good. You did not need to study the Sonata with me first. The finger was just meant to prove my attentiveness.' Later Beethoven had to play, and chose the D Minor Sonata [Op. 31 No. 2], which had just appeared. The Princess, who was expecting that Beethoven would surely make a mistake somewhere, now placed herself behind him while I turned the pages. At bars 53 and 54, Beethoven missed the beginning and instead of going down two notes and then two more, struck with his whole hand all the crotchets (3–4 notes at the same time) while descending; it sounded as if a piano were being cleaned out. The Princess gave him several not exactly gentle slaps on the head with the observation, 'If the pupil gets one finger for one wrong note, the Master must be punished with the whole hand for making bad mistakes.' Everyone laughed, and Beethoven first. He started again and played wonderfully. Particularly the Adagio he played inimitably. WRBN 92.

Anton Schindler on the Sonate Pathétique:

What the *Sonate Pathétique* was in the hands of Beethoven (although he left something to be desired as regards clean playing), was something that one had to have heard, and heard again, in order to be quite certain that it was the same already well-known work. Above all, every single thing became, in his hands, a new creation, wherein his always *legato* playing, one of the particular characteristics of his execution, formed an important part. In his lessons, Beethoven taught: always place the hands on the keyboard so that the fingers do not rise any more than is strictly necessary, for only with this method is it possible to create a tone and to learn how to 'sing'. He hated staccato playing, especially in the execution of passages; he called it 'finger dance' or 'leading the hands into the air'. The pieces which I myself heard Beethoven execute were, with few exceptions, always quite free of tempo limitations: a *tempo rubato* in the truest sense of the word, according to the demands of the contents and situation, without, however, the slightest tendency to caricature. It was the clearest and most comprehensible declamation, in the utmost degree, as perhaps can only be elicited from his works.

His older friends, who carefully followed the evolution of his spirit in every aspect, assure [me] that he developed this style of execution in the first years of the third period of his life, and that he turned completely away from his earlier manner of playing with fewer *nuances*. From this it is clear that his urge towards discovery had already found the ways and means to open up with confidence the portals of the mystery to both laity and initiated.

He wanted the quartets to be performed in the same manner as the sonatas, for they paint states of mind, as do the majority of his sonatas. Kerst II, 32.

Ignaz Moscheles on the Sonate Pathétique:

At this time I heard from some of my fellow pupils that a young composer had arrived in Vienna who wrote the most extraordinary stuff, which no one could either play or understand; a Baroque music in conflict with all the rules. This composer's name was Beethoven. When I went back to the circulating library in order to satisfy my curiosity about the eccentric genius who bore that name, I found Beethoven's *Sonate Pathétique*. That was in 1804. Since my pocket money did not suffice to buy it, I secretly copied it out. The novelty of the style fascinated me, and I was seized by such an enthusiastic admiration of it that I went so far as to forget myself and tell my teacher about my new discovery. This gentleman reminded me of his instructions and warned me against playing or studying eccentric productions before I had developed a style based on more respectable models. Without paying heed to his instructions, however, I laid Beethoven's works on the piano, in the order of their appearance, and found in them such consolation and pleasure as no other composer ever vouchsafed me.
TDR II, 146.

Count von Keglevics writes about his aunt, Princess Odescalchi:

The Sonata [Op. 7] was composed for her by Beethoven when she was still a girl. He had the whim – one of many – since he lived across from her, of coming to give her lessons clad in a dressing-gown, slippers and a peaked nightcap. TDR II, 52.

Letter from Beethoven to Zmeskall:

[Vienna, about 1801]
I write to you, my dear Music Count, on the best paper I have, that you will be so kind as to play the Septet tomorrow at Odescalchi's. Schindleker is not in town, the whole performance would have to be abandoned if you do not play and I would certainly fall under the suspicion of having been remiss about something.

Therefore, I beg you, dear M.G. [Musikgraf] not to fail me in this favour. You will surely be treated with the greatest consideration. Prince Odescalchi will write to you personally tomorrow morning.

The rehearsal is tomorrow morning at eleven o'clock. I will send you the score so that you can look over the solo in the last Minuet which, as you know, is the most difficult. Eppinger will play the violin.

– I await you –
Your Bthvn.

KAL 80. Anderson 56.

43 Johann Joseph Prince von Liechtenstein; oil portrait by J. B. Lampi the Elder.

44 Josepha Princess von Liechtenstein was a
pupil of Beethoven's; oil portrait by
Angelika Kauffmann.

45 Innocenzo Prince d'Erba Odescalchi;
anonymous oil portrait.

46 Anna Louisa Barbara (Babette) Princess
Odescalchi; anonymous oil portrait.

Beethoven's oldest Viennese patron, Prince Carl Lichnowsky, had a younger brother, Count Moritz, also a pupil of Mozart's, who soon became not only a staunch patron but also a firm friend; the friendship lasted the whole of Beethoven's life. Altogether it is significant how Beethoven managed to be on terms of near equality with the Austro-Hungarian aristocracy; this was partly because they thought that the 'van' in Beethoven's name denoted nobility and thus considered him one of theirs, but also because Beethoven always insisted on being treated as an intellectual equal. It should be stressed that, at this period in Beethoven's life, towards the end of the eighteenth century, he presented a well-manicured appearance and dressed very neatly in the style of the period; he was also an interesting talker, and, unlike most musicians of the period, fascinated by politics. He also must have had considerable personal charm, such as a later letter to Count Moritz (1814) well illustrates.

Anton Schindler about Count Moritz von Lichnowsky:

Even higher stood his [Carl Lichnowsky's] brother Count Moritz Lichnowsky, also Mozart's pupil, who must be described as the most faithful companion of Beethoven during his whole life.
Schindler I, 21.

Letter from Beethoven to Count Moritz von Lichnowsky:

Baden, 21 September 1841 [1814]

Worthy and esteemed Count
and friend,

Unfortunately I received your letter only yesterday. Many thanks for thinking of me and also all good wishes to the honoured Princess Christiane [Thun-Lichnowsky]. Yesterday, I took a beautiful walk in the Brühl with a friend and in the course of our amicable conversation you were a frequent subject and lo! yesterday evening on arriving home I found your good letter. I see that you are constantly overwhelming me with kindnesses. As I should not like you to imagine that any step I have taken was dictated by a new interest or, indeed, anything of that sort, I hasten to tell you that a Sonata of mine will shortly appear which I have dedicated to you. I had wanted to surprise you, for this dedication has been long destined for you. But your letter of yesterday obliges me to reveal it to you now. There is no need of any new motive for me to express openly my feelings for your friendship and goodwill. But by anything resembling, even in the slightest, a gift you would cause me much distress because then you would have completely misunderstood my intention. Anything of that kind I can only refuse.

I kiss the hands of the Princess (in gratitude) for her rememberance and goodwill towards me. I have never forgotten to what an extent I am

<u>indebted to you</u>, even though an unfortunate event resulted in a situation in which I was not able to express it as I should have wished. . . .

Farewell,
my honoured friend
and regard me as
ever worthy of your goodwill –
your

I kiss the hands of the beloved   Beethoven.
Princess C. a thousand times.
KFR 209. Anderson 498.

> In 1798, Beethoven made another successful concert trip to Prague where he played the Piano Concerto in B Flat, Op. 19, perhaps with the revised finale that we know today rather than the original Rondo (WoO 6). It is also considered possible that he gave at Prague the first performance of the Piano Concerto in C, Op. 15, which, despite its earlier opus number, is the later of the two works.
>
> Beethoven's first big public concert in Vienna took place on 2 April 1800, and included the first performance of the First Symphony and perhaps the Viennese première of the Piano Concerto in C, Op. 15. The Symphony was dedicated to Baron Gottfried van Swieten, one of those in Vienna who immediately recognized Beethoven's enormous talents. The concert also included the now famous Septet, dedicated to the Empress Marie Therese herself. Emperor Francis was never an admirer of Beethoven, but so long as Marie Therese was still alive, Beethoven managed to preserve a tenuous connection with the Royal and Imperial house. The concert, which took place at the Burgtheater, was a decided success: Beethoven was now, after Haydn, the leading composer in Vienna.

The Allgemeine Musikalische Zeitung *reviews Beethoven's concert on 2 April 1800:*

Finally, Herr Beethoven was able for once to obtain the use of the theatre, and this was the most interesting Academy held for a long time. He played a new concerto of his own composition which contains many beautiful things, namely the first two movements. Then a septet by him was performed, it is written with a great deal of taste and feeling. He then improvised with mastery, and at the close a symphony of his composition was performed, which revealed much art, novelty and wealth of ideas. But there was too much use of wind instruments, so that it sounded more like a wind-band than an orchestra. Perhaps we might do some good if we make the following observations on the subject of this Academy. The orchestra of the Italian Opera showed to very poor advantage. First: quarrels regarding the conductors. Beethoven believed, and rightly, that rather than Herr Conti no one could be better trusted to

47 Moritz Count Lichnowsky, younger brother of Prince Carl (ill. 30); anonymous oil portrait.

48 Marie Therese, Empress of Austria; oil portrait by J. Kreutzinger.

49 The old Burgtheater in the Michaelerplatz, Vienna; coloured engraving by Carl Postl, 1810. Beethoven gave his first public benefit concert here on 2 April 1800.

conduct than Herr Wranitzky. The gentlemen did not want to play under him. The shortcomings of this orchestra, already denounced above, were therefore even more evident, especially since B.'s composition is hard to play. In the accompaniments they did not take the trouble to consider the soloist. Of delicacy in accompanying, of following the sequence of the feelings of the solo player and so forth, not the slightest trace. In the second part of the symphony they were so condescending that they did not even follow the beat, so that it was impossible to get any life into their playing, especially in the woodwinds. In such cases, of what avail is their skill? – which one does not in the least wish to deny to the majority of the members of this Association. What significant effect can even the most excellent composition achieve?
TDR II, 172.

Johann Nepomuk Emanuel Dolezalek reports on the Emperor Francis I:

The Emperor Francis did not wish to hear anything about Beethoven's music: 'There is something revolutionary in that music!'
Kerst II, 192.

Cipriani Potter about Beethoven:

Once, when he, Potter, told Beethoven of the effect which the Septet had at that time on him, Beethoven said, more or less: 'In those days I did not know how to compose. Now, I think I do know.' On this, or on a similar occasion, he said, 'Now I shall write something better' – and soon after appeared the B-Flat Sonata, Opus 106, the work of the year 1818.
TDR IV, 57. (Potter was numbered among Beethoven's admirers.)

Letter from Baron Gottfried van Swieten to Beethoven:

[undated]
To Herr Beethoven, in the Alstergasse No. 45, care of Prince Lichnowsky.
    If next Wednesday you are not prevented, I should like to see you, with your nightcap in your pocket, at my house at half-past-eight in the evening. Please do not fail to give me an answer.

Swieten.

From Beethoven's diary
[October or November 1793]:
Ate yesterday evening at Swieten's – tip of a 17th; to the porter for opening the door, 4 Kreutzer.
TDR I, 360.

50 Baron Gottfried van Swieten, son of Maria Theresa's private physician, was director of the Imperial and Royal Court Library and also a composer, to whom Beethoven dedicated his Symphony No. 1 in C, Op. 21 (silhouette by P. Gonord, 1781).

51 The National Library on the Josephsplatz, Vienna, where Baron van Swieten had a flat (coloured engraving by Carl Schütz, 1780).

Anton Schindler writes about Beethoven's obstinacy:

Beethoven very often ran his head against the wall. . . . Even van Swieten's understanding advice and admonitions often went unheeded. He, who had been his sponsor in high society, had to be satisfied if the capricious artist consented to appear at his musical evenings. Emancipation from all the conventions of the drawing-room seems to have been one of his early obsessions, although his personal relations, in particular his close connections with the élite of the musical world who, overlooking his social shortcomings, regarded him as one of themselves, should have been sufficient grounds for him to lay such aspirations aside, at least for a short time.   Schindler I, 23.

Gottfried van Swieten writes about himself:

Insofar as music is concerned, I have returned altogether to those times when it was considered necessary to study an art soundly and thoroughly before practising it. In this conviction I find nourishment for both spirit and heart: and this gives me strength when I have been cast down by further evidence of the decline of the arts. My comforters are, above all, Handel and the Bachs and, along with them, those few masters of our present day who, following with a firm tread the path of those examples of truth and greatness, promise to reach their goal, or have already reached it.   *Allgemeine Musikalische Zeitung,* Leipzig, No. 16, 3 January 1799.

Carl Czerny writes about his first meeting with Beethoven:

I still remember how one day Gelinek told my father that he had been asked that evening to compete with a foreign piano-player at a reception. 'We must make mincemeat out of him,' added Gelinek. The next day my father asked Gelinek for the outcome of the previous day's duel.

'Oh,' said Gelinek quite subdued, 'I'll never forget yesterday evening! Satan himself is hidden in that young man. I have never heard anyone play like that! He improvised on a theme which I gave him as I never heard even Mozart improvise. Then he played some of his own compositions which are in the highest degree remarkable and magnificent. He can overcome difficulties and draw effects from the piano such as we couldn't even allow ourselves to dream about.'

'Eh,' said my father, 'and what is the man's name?'

'He is', answered Gelinek, 'a small, ugly, black and wild-looking young man whom Prince Lichnowsky brought here a few years ago from Germany in order to have him study with Haydn, Albrechtsberger and Salieri; his name is Beethoven.'. . .

I was about ten years old when I was taken to Beethoven through the kind offices of Krumpholz. It was the winter of 1799–1800. How I was overjoyed and terrified on the day when I was to meet the esteemed master! Even today [1842] every moment of it is still fresh in my memory. On a winter's day, my father, Krumpholz and I walked from the Leopold-stadt, where we still lived, into the city, to the so-called Tiefer Graben [the name of a street], climbed up, as if in a tower, to the fifth or sixth floor, where a rather grubby-looking servant announced us to Beethoven and then showed us in. A very barren-looking room, papers and clothes strewn all over the place, a few boxes, bare walls, hardly a single chair save for a rickety one by the Fortepiano, a Walter, at that time the best make. In this room were gathered six to eight persons, including both the brothers Wranitzky, Süssmeyer, Schuppanzigh and one of Beet-hoven's brothers.

Beethoven himself was dressed in a jacket of some shaggy dark grey cloth and trousers of the same material, so that he immediately reminded me of Campe's *Robinson Crusoe*,★ which I had just then read. The coal-black hair cut *à la Titus* stood up around his head. His black beard, un-shaven for several days, darkened the lower part of his already dark-complexioned face. Also I noticed at a glance, as children are wont to do, that his ears were stuffed with cotton-wool which seemed to have been dipped in some yellow fluid. Yet at that time not the slightest sign of deafness was apparent. I had to play something immediately, and since I was too shy to begin with one of his own compositions, I played Mozart's great C Major Concerto [K. 503] which begins with chords. Beethoven was immediately attentive; he came close to my chair and played with his left hand the orchestra part in those sections where I had only accompanying passages. His hands were very hairy and his fingers, especially at the tips, very broad. He expressed himself as being satisfied, so I made bold and played the *Pathétique* Sonata which had then just appeared, and finally the *Adelaide* which my father sang with his very good tenor voice. When I had finished, Beethoven turned to my father and said, 'The boy has talent. I will teach him myself and accept him as my pupil. Send him to me a few times a week. Before anything else, obtain for him Emanuel Bach's handbook on the proper way to play the clavier, so that he can bring it with him the next time he comes.'

★ The German writer Joachim Heinrich Campe (1746–1816) wrote a version of *Robinson Crusoe* based on Defoe.

In the first lessons, Beethoven gave me scales in every key, showed me the only proper position of the hands and of the fingers and particularly the use of the thumb, then unknown to the majority of players, rules whose complete scope I mastered only at a much later time.

Then he went over the exercises of the handbook with me and drew my special attention to *legato* of which he himself was an unequalled master and which, at that time, all other pianists believed to be impossible to obtain on the Fortepiano. At that time, dating still from Mozart's days, the clipped and *staccato* way of playing was the fashion.

Czerny 10 f. (Paul [1756–1808] and Anton [1761–1819] Wranitzky were both composers; so was F. X. Süssmayer [*recte*], a former pupil of Mozart's.)

Beethoven was never entirely free from ill health; the latest generation of Beethoven scholars believes that he probably caught syphilis, and in any case he was always subject to intestinal disorders, sometimes of considerable severity. But towards the end of the eighteenth century, Beethoven began to discover something much more frightful, namely that he was losing his hearing. Gradually, indeed, Beethoven became stone deaf over the years, and it can be imagined how the awareness of this increasing deafness affected him. From the psychological standpoint it is interesting to observe that at the very depth of his misery, when he was writing the 'Heiligenstädter Testament' of 1802, he was composing the brilliant and energetic Second Symphony; this should be something of a warning to those who will insist on seeing a constant parallel between Beethoven's life and his music. We do not need to go so far as W. H. Auden in condemning Beethoven's letters, but it is obvious that his music always existed on a higher level, often isolated from his physical and mental agonies.

Letters from Beethoven to Dr Franz Gerhard Wegeler in Bonn:

Vienna, 29 June [1801]

My dear, good Wegeler,

... You want to know about my situation: Well on the whole it is not so bad. Since last year Lichnowsky, however difficult it will be for you to believe it when I tell you, who was always and still is my warmest friend (there have been small misunderstandings but have these not further cemented our friendship?), has placed at my disposal a fixed sum of 600 Florins on which I may draw so long as I do not obtain a suitable appointment. My compositions bring in a considerable amount, and I can truthfully say that I receive more offers of commissions than I can possibly accept. Moreover, for every composition I have six or seven publishers and could have more if I should want them. People no longer bargain with me: I state my price and they pay. So you see that this is an agreeable state of affairs. For example, I see a friend in need, and if the state of my purse will not allow me to help him out on the spot, I have only to sit down at my desk and in a short time help for him is forthcoming. I have also become more economical than formerly. If I should settle here permanently it would certainly soon be possible for me to obtain one day each year for a concert; I have already given a few. Only that jealous demon, namely my bad health, has thrown a mean spoke in my wheel; in the past three years my hearing has become increasingly weaker. It appears that my abdomen which, as you know, was already at that time [in Bonn] in a wretched state, has become worse here. I have been constantly plagued by colic and hence by a fearful fatigue. This appears to have been the original cause of my deafness. Frank wanted to build up the tone of my body by means of strong tonic medicines, and my hearing with almond oil. But Prosit! it did me no good whatever. My hearing became even worse and the digestive trouble remained the same. This went on all last year until the autumn when sometimes I was reduced to utter despair. Then a medical asinus recommended cold baths for my condition; a more intelligent one suggested the usual tepid Danube baths. These worked wonders. I improved, but my deafness persisted or even worsened. This winter I was really wretched. I had fearful colics and I again relapsed completely into my former state. This went on until about four weeks ago, when I went to Vering, since I began to think that this condition might call for a surgeon and, anyway, I always had confidence in him. He succeeded in almost checking the violent diarrhoea. He prescribed the tepid Danube baths into which I must pour a flask of strengthening substances. He gave me no medicines until about four days ago when he prescribed four pills daily for the stomach and an infusion for my ear. I must say that now I find myself stronger and better. Only my ears hum and buzz continuously day and night. I can tell you that I lead a miserable existence. For the past two years I avoid almost all social intercourse because it is impossible for me to say to people: 'I am deaf.' If I practised any other profession it would be easier, but in my profession this is a terrible condition. My enemies, and their number is not small – what would they not say! To give you an idea of this remarkable deafness, I can tell you that at the theatre I must find a place very close to the orchestra in order to understand the actors. If I am a little way distant I cannot hear the upper notes of the voices or of the instruments. In conversation it is remarkable that there are people who have never noticed this. Since I am often given to periods of distraction, people attribute my deafness to this. Sometimes, if someone speaks in a low voice, I can barely understand; I hear the

52 Portrait of Beethoven that was sold by Artaria & Co.; engraving by J. Neidl from a drawing by G. E. Stainhauser von Treuberg, 1800.

sounds but not the words. If anyone shouts it is unbearable. What is to become of me, heaven only knows. Vering says that I will undoubtedly improve, even if I am not completely cured. I have cursed my fate many times already. Plutarch has shown me the way to resignation. I shall, if it is at all possible, challenge my fate, although there will be moments when I shall be God's most unhappy creature. I beg you to tell no one of this condition of mine, not even Lorchen. What I tell you is a secret which I entrust to your keeping. I should like you to correspond with Vering about this. If my condition goes on like this, I will come to you next spring. Rent a house for me in some beautiful place in the country and then I will become a peasant for half a year. Perhaps that will change things. Resignation! What a wretched means of escape, and yet that is the only thing left to me. You will surely forgive me if I unload on you the troubles of your friend, when you are yourself in a sorrowful condition of your own. Steffen Breuning is here at present and we see each other almost daily. It does me so much good to revive the old feelings of friendship. . . .

[I send] you the portrait . . . of your ever good and affectionate Beethoven; it is being published by Artaria who has often, like many others, including art shops, requested it from me.

KAL 45 ff. Anderson 51.

Countess Josephine von Deym writes to her sisters:

[Vienna, 10 December 1800]
. . . Yesterday we had music to honour the Duchess. I had to play and was, moreover, responsible for all the arrangements and supposed to see that everything went off well. We opened all the doors and everything was illuminated. I assure you, it was a splendid sight. Beethoven played the Sonata with violoncello, I played the last of the three violin Sonatas [Op. 12] accompanied by Schuppanzigh who, like all the others, played divinely. Then Beethoven, that real angel, let us hear his new Quartets [Op. 18], which have not been engraved yet. and are the greatest of their kind. The famous Kraft played cello, Schuppanzigh first violin. You can imagine what a treat it was for us! The Duchess was enchanted and everything went famously.

La Mara, *op cit.*, p. 14. (The Duchess Julia von Giovane, née Freiin von Mudersbach, lived at the Deyms' house in the Rotenturmstrasse. For the Deym family, see pp. 97 ff.)

The Allgemeine Musikalische Zeitung *reports on the Augarten Concerts, 1804:*

The second subscription of our Augarten Concerts opened in a very brilliant fashion . . . The concert began with Beethoven's great Symphony in D Major, a work full of new and original ideas, of great vigour, effective instrumentation and erudite development. It would undoubtedly gain, however, by the curtailment of a few sections as well as the sacrifice of certain far too unusual modulations. This Symphony was followed by a Concerto by Beethoven in C Minor. . . . This Concerto without doubt belongs among Beethoven's most beautiful compositions. It is worked out in a masterly fashion. Herr Ries, who took the solo part, is, at present, Beethoven's only pupil and his most fervent admirer. He had prepared the piece entirely under the direction of his teacher and gave proof of a very smooth expressive execution as well as unusual polish and sureness, overcoming with ease the most extraordinary difficulties.

Allgemeine Musikalische Zeitung, Leipzig, No. 46, 15 August 1804.

53 Johann Nepomuk Hummel, a well-known pianist and composer who had been a pupil of Mozart. As a pianist he became a serious rival of Beethoven's with the Viennese public (anonymous oil portrait, c. 1814).

Ferdinand Ries, son of the first violin of the Bonn orchestra, came to Vienna to study with Beethoven. He later collaborated with Beethoven's old friend Wegeler in writing a short biographical sketch of his experiences with Beethoven which gives many interesting eye-witness accounts of the composer.

Ferdinand Ries describes Beethoven as a teacher:

Beethoven gave me his beautiful Concerto in C Minor (Op. 37) while still in manuscript, so that I might appear with it for the first time in public as his pupil. In fact I am the only person who appeared under this guise during his lifetime.

Besides myself he recognized only the Archduke Rudolph as a pupil. Beethoven himself conducted, and probably no concerto was ever so beautifully accompanied. We had two main rehearsals. I had begged Beethoven to compose a cadenza for me, which he refused to do and directed me to write one myself which he would then correct. Beethoven was very satisfied with my composition and made very few changes. Only there was an extremely brilliant and difficult passage in it which he liked but which seemed to him to be rather risky; he therefore told me to write another one. Eight days before the performance he asked to hear the cadenza again. I played it and bungled the passage. He advised me again, albeit somewhat unwillingly, to change it. I did so, but the

54 Ferdinand Ries, son of the first violinist in the Elector's orchestra at Bonn, studied piano with Beethoven in Vienna from 1801 to 1805 (anonymous oil portrait).

55, 56 Moritz Count von Fries and his wife Therese; pastels by Anette von Eckhardt after drawings by C. Vogel, 1813. Fries, an artistically minded banker, and his beautiful wife were patrons of Beethoven, who dedicated many works to the Count.

new one did not satisfy me. So I practised the other one diligently without, however, being too certain of it. In the public concert, during the cadenza, Beethoven sat down quietly. I could not persuade myself to choose the easier one. When I boldly began the difficult one, Beethoven made a violent start with his chair. But nevertheless it came off perfectly and Beethoven was so pleased that he cried 'Bravo' aloud. This electrified the whole audience and immediately assured me of a standing among the artists. Later, when he expressed his satisfaction over my performance, he added, 'Obstinate you certainly are! If you had bungled the passage I would never have given you another lesson!'
WRBN 113.

Ferdinand Ries recalls Beethoven's duel with the pianist Daniel Steibelt:

When Steibelt arrived in Vienna armed with his great Parisian reputation, many of Beethoven's friends were worried for fear he might injure Beethoven's reputation.

Steibelt did not call on him. They first met one evening at Count Fries' where Beethoven played for the first time his new Trio in B-Flat for piano, clarinet and violoncello (Opus 11). In this work the pianist cannot show himself off to any great advantage. Steibelt listened to it with a certain air of condescension, paid a few compliments and felt himself certain of victory. He played a Quintet of his own composition, improvised and also made a great effect with his *tremulandos* which, at that time, constituted a great novelty. Beethoven could not be induced to

play any more. Eight days later there was another concert at Count Fries. Steibelt again played a quintet with much success and in addition (and this was quite evident) had prepared a brilliant improvisation, choosing as a theme the subject of the variations of Beethoven's Trio. This outraged not only Beethoven's supporters but also the composer himself. He now had to seat himself at the piano in order to improvise. He went in his usual, I must say ungracious, manner to the instrument as if half lunging towards it, grabbing, as he passed, the violoncello part of Steibelt's quintet, placed it (intentionally?) upside-down on the music stand and from the opening notes drummed out a theme with one finger. Offended and stimulated at the same time, he improvised in such a manner that Steibelt left the room before Beethoven had finished. He refused ever to meet him again; in fact he made it a condition that Beethoven should not be invited anywhere where his company was requested.

WRBN 81 f.

Carl Czerny describes Beethoven's improvisation in Cock's London Musical Miscellany, *1852* [*English original*]:

His improvisation was most brilliant and striking – in whatever company he might chance to be he knew how to achieve such an effect upon every listener, that frequently not an eye remained dry, while many would break out into loud sobs, for there was something wonderful in his expression in addition to the beauty and originality of his ideas and the

77

57 Soirée in the palace of Moritz Count von Fries in Vienna;
drawing by J. Fischer, 1800.

spirited style of rendering them. After ending an improvisation of this
kind, he would burst into loud laughter and banter his hearers on the
emotion he had caused in them. 'You are fools' he would say. Sometimes
he would feel himself <u>insulted</u> by these indications of sympathy.
'Who can live among such spoiled children' he would cry and only on
that account (as he told me) he declined to accept an invitation which the
King of Prussia gave him after one of the extempory performances
above described.

TDR II, 14.

*Letters from Georg August Griesinger to Court Councillor Böttiger in Dresden,
on the subject of Count Fries:*

Vienna, 25 September 1811.
Countess Fries had prepared an entertainment for her husband on the
day of St Maurice at Lengbach, where I stayed for a few days. Since
Fries, however, only returned from Styria yesterday, richer by a
beautiful manor which he had purchased there, the feast at Lengbach
will therefore be celebrated tomorrow and I cannot possibly fail to
honour this charming and precious friend with my presence. . . .

Vienna, 1 September 1819.

. . . Yesterday the solemn burial of Countess Fries took place in Vöslau. The procession first moved to the neighbouring church in Gainfahrn . . . where every step reminded me of the happiest hours. Count Fries left today with his children for Styria. Seclusion, occupation and smiling surrounding are the most effective cure after such a shock. . . .

Autograph. Sächsische Landesbibliothek, Dresden.

In 1801, Beethoven had an opportunity to display his talents in quite a new and different way: the composition of a full-length ballet, *Die Geschöpfe des Prometheus* (also known as *Die Menschen des Prometheus*). This is a ravishingly beautiful score and although the ballet was considered problematical, Beethoven's music had a considerable success when it was first performed at the Burgtheater on 28 March 1801.

Aloys Fuchs reports in the Wiener Allgemeine Musik-Zeitung *(No. 39, 1846) on Beethoven's meeting with Haydn:*

It has long been known, and especially proven by certain remarks by Beethoven against his equally artistic colleague Goethe, that Beethoven was very much aware of his position in the world of music, and on certain occasions knew how to take advantage of it, even if it meant running the risk of being harshly judged or misunderstood by lay persons. . . . When in 1801 Beethoven had written the music to the ballet *The Creatures of Prometheus*, he encountered his former teacher, the great Joseph Haydn, who immediately stopped him and said, 'Now, yesterday I heard your ballet and it pleased me very much.' Beethoven thereupon answered, 'Oh, my dear Papa, you are very kind, but it is a long way from being a "Creation".' Haydn, surprised and almost offended by this answer, said after a short silence, 'That is true, it is not yet a "Creation" and I very much doubt whether it will ever succeed in being one.' Whereupon each of them, somewhat dumbfounded, took leave of the other.

Kerst I, 108.

The Historisches Taschenbuch *reports on Beethoven's* Prometheus *(1801):*

A Ballet, the *Men of Prometheus* [sic] did not please, although the music of that profound genius, Beethoven, contains much that is beautiful, even if it is not always particularly suited to the dance. . . .

Hist. Tb. I, 236f.

From the Diary of Joseph Carl Rosenbaum:

Friday, the 27th [March 1801]. Cold and cloudy. Quite dark. I went early to the office and to the rehearsal of the ballet, *The Creatures of Prometheus*, of Sala Viganò. Music by Beethoven. . . . The ballet did not please at all, the music a little . . . at the end the ballet was more hissed then applauded.

HJB V, 92. (Rosenbaum, married to the singer Therese Gassmann and a close acquaintance of Haydn, was no admirer of Beethoven.)

In 1800, the beautiful young Giulietta, Countess Guicciardi, took Viennese society by storm. She became Beethoven's pupil and he fell in love with her. The match was, of course, hopeless because of the difference in their ranks, but the beautiful countess has been immortalized as the recipient of perhaps the most famous piano sonata ever written, the so-called 'Moonlight' Sonata in C-sharp Minor, Op. 27, No. 2. Giulietta married a third-rate composer of ballets, Robert Count von Gallenberg, and the couple thereafter left Vienna to settle in Naples, where, incidentally, Countess Gallenberg carried on a love affair with Prince Hermann von Pückler-Muskau. Her marriage with Gallenberg was, in any case, a disastrous failure. Part of the desperation of the 'Heiligenstädter Testament' is certainly the result of Beethoven's broken love affair with Countess Giulietta.

Countess Josephine von Deym writes to her sisters:

[January 1801]

. . . Julie Guicciardi is creating a furore here. They refer to her only as the beautiful Guicciardi, and you know that she understands how to capitalize on it. She is intimate with the Gallenbergs.

La Mara, *op. cit.*, p. 14.

Letter from Beethoven to Dr Franz Gerhard Wegeler:

Vienna, 16 November [1801]

. . . I am now living a more agreeable life, inasmuch as I go about more among my fellow men. You can hardly imagine how empty, how sad my life has been for the past two years. My weak hearing haunted me everywhere, like a ghost, and so I avoided people. I must have appeared like a misanthrope, and yet I am so far from being one. This change has been brought about by a lovable charming girl who loves me and whom I love. So after two years I enjoy a few happy moments and this is the first time I feel that marriage could bring happiness with it. Unfortunately she is not of my class – and now – I naturally could not marry – I must somehow keep going as best I can. . . .

KAL 53. Anderson 54.

58 Giulietta Countess Guicciardi, later Countess von Gallenberg; anonymous miniature on ivory found after Beethoven's death among his effects. He was passionately in love with Giulietta, who was seventeen when she became his pupil, and he was profoundly shocked by her marriage.

Anton Schindler's sister, Frau Egloff, speaks to Ludwig Nohl:

She [Countess Gallenberg] was not happy. What woman could be, with a husband like that. She lived always a very retired life in the same house with her husband, by whom she had several children, but they saw each other only at the table.

A. Chr. Kalischer, *Beethoven und Seine Zeitgenossen: Beethoven's Frauenkreis*, Berlin 1909, I, 184 ff.

From Beethoven's conversation books [original partly French]:

February 1823

[Beethoven:] I was very much loved by her, far more than her husband ever was – [there follows a cancelled passage] – he was really more her lover than I was. But from her I heard about his poverty and I found a rich man who gave me 500 florins to help him out.

[Beethoven:] He was always my enemy and that is the reason why I did him all the good that I could.

[Schindler:] Whereupon he also said to me, 'He is an intolerable man', undoubtedly out of sheer gratitude. But, Father, forgive them, for they know not what they do!

Madame the Countess? ·

Was she rich?

She has a pretty face, down to here!

Mons. G[allenberg].

Is it a long time since she was married to Mons. de Gallenberg?

[Beethoven:] She was born Guicciardi.

She was already his wife before [she went to] Italy, and she came to see me in tears, but I spurned her.

Hercules at the crossroads.

If I had wanted to spend my strength and my life in this manner, what would have been left over for the nobler better part?

Konv. Sch. II, 363. Autograph in the Berlin State Library.

Countess Giulietta Gallenberg's recollections about Beethoven recorded by Otto Jahn (1852):

Beethoven was her teacher. He allowed her to play his compositions, but was exceedingly severe with her until the interpretation was correct to the very last tiny detail. He insisted on a light touch. He himself was often violent, throwing the music around and tearing it up. He refused payment, although he was very poor. But he would accept linen, under the pretext that the Countess herself had sewed it. He also taught Countess Odescalchi and Baroness Ertmann. His pupils either went to him, or he came to them. He did not like to play his own compositions, but he would improvise. At the slightest disturbance he would get up and go away. Count Brunswik, who played the violoncello, adored him, as did also his sisters Therese and Countess Deym. Beethoven had given the Rondo in G [Op. 51, No. 2] to Countess Gallenberg Guicciardi, but asked for it back because he had to dedicate something to Countess Lichnowsky, and then dedicated to her the Sonata [Op. 27, No. 2]. Beethoven was very ugly, but noble, sensitive and cultured. Most of the time he was shabbily dressed.

TDR II, 307. (For Princess [*recte*] Odescalchi and Baroness Ertmann, see pp. 56 and 103 ff.)

Beethoven's Will written at Heiligenstadt:

For my brothers Carl and [Johann] Beethoven.

O ye men, who consider or declare me to be hostile, obstinate or misanthropic, how unjust you are to me, for you do not know the secret cause of that which makes me seem so to you. My heart and my soul,

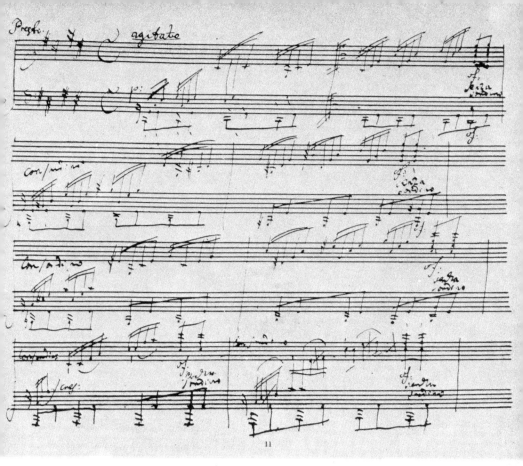

59 Autograph page of the 'Moonlight' Sonata (*Sonata quasi una Fantasia*, Op. 27 No. 2), dedicated to Countess Giulietta Guicciardi.

since my childhood, have ever been filled with tender feelings of good will: I was even ready to perform great deeds. But consider that for six years now I have been afflicted with an incurable condition, made worse by incompetent physicians, deceived for year after year by the hope of an improvement and now obliged to face the prospect of a permanent disability [cancelled word] (the healing of which may take years or may even prove to be quite impossible). Born with an ardent, lively temperament and also inclined to the distractions of society, I was, at an early age, obliged to seclude myself and to live my life in solitude. If, once in a while, I attempted to ignore all this, oh, how harshly would I be driven back by the doubly sad experience of my bad hearing; yet it was not possible for me to say: speak louder, shout, because I am deaf.

Alas, how would it be possible for me to admit to a weakness of the one sense that should be perfect to a higher degree in me than in others, the one sense which I once possessed in the highest perfection, a perfection that few others of my profession have ever possessed. No, I cannot do it. So forgive me if you see me draw back from your company which I would so gladly share. My misfortune is doubly hard to bear, inasmuch as I will surely be misunderstood. For me there can be no recreation in the society of others, no intelligent conversation, no mutual exchange of ideas; only as much as is required by the most pressing needs can I venture into society. I am obliged to live like an outcast. If I venture into the company of men, I am overcome by a burning terror, inasmuch as I fear to find myself in the danger of allowing my condition to be noticed. So it has been for this last half year which I have spent in the country. Advised by my sensible physician to spare my hearing as much as possible, he [only: erased] to a certain extent encouraged my natural disposition: although sometimes torn by the desire for companionship, I allowed myself to be tempted into it. But what a humiliation when someone standing next to me could hear from the distance the sound of a flute whereas I heard nothing. Or, someone could hear the shepherd singing, and that also I did not hear. Such experiences brought me near to despair, it would have needed little for me to put an end to my life. It was art only which held me back. Ah, it seemed to me to be impossible to leave the world before I had brought forth all that I felt destined to bring forth. So I endured this miserable existence – miserable indeed. For I have so sensitive a body that even a slight change can transport me from the highest to the most wretched states. Patience – it is said – is what I must now choose as my guide. This I have done – and I hope that my resolution will remain firm until the implacable Parcae are pleased to break the thread. Perhaps my condition will improve, perhaps it will not. I am obliged – when only in my twenty-eighth year – to become a philosopher, and that is not easy, and for an artist it is harder than for any other. Almighty God, Thou lookest down into my innermost being; Thou knowest that the love of mankind and the desire to do good dwell therein. Oh men, when you once shall read this, reflect then, that you have wronged me, and let some unfortunate be comforted that he has found one like himself who, in the face of all the obstacles which nature has placed in his path, has yet done all that lay in his power to be numbered among the ranks of worthy artists and men – You, my brothers Carl and [Johann], as soon as I am dead, if Professor Schmid[t] be still alive, request him in my name to describe my malady, and let him attach this written document to the report of my ailment [an illegible word: erased], so that, as far as possible, the world will be reconciled with me after my death. At the same time I hereby declare both of you to be [my: crossed out] the heirs of my small estate (if such it can be termed), divide it justly, bear with and help each other. What harm you have done to me, that, you know, has long since been forgiven. I thank you, my brother Carl in particular, for the affection which you have shown me in these latter times. My wish is that [I: crossed out] you may lead a better life and one more [full of: crossed out] free of care than mine. Recommend virtue to your [after: crossed out] children: that alone, and not money, can ensure happiness. I speak from experience: it was virtue which sustained me in my misery; next I thank my art that I did not end my life by suicide. Farewell – love each other. I thank all my friends, in particular Prince Lichnowski and Professor Schmidt. I wish the instruments from Prince L. to be preserved by one of you, but no quarrel between you should arise over them. In the event that they might serve a more useful purpose, sell them by all means. How happy I am if even in my grave I can be of help to you. So it has come to pass. I go to meet death joyfully. If it comes before I have had the opportunity to fulfil all my artistic destiny, then, despite my hard fate, it shall have come too soon, and I shall wish that it had come later. Nevertheless, I shall be content, for will it not free me from a condition of endless suffering? Come when thou willst, I go bravely to meet thee. Farewell, and do not forget me wholly. I deserve it from you, since in life I have often given thought of how to make you happy. Be ye so.

Ludwig van Beethoven.

Seal

Heiglnstadt [sic]
on 6th October,
1802.

60 View of Heiligenstadt, the spa where Beethoven spent the summer of 1802; coloured line etching by Maria Geissler, c. 1800.

[on the last, 4th page]

Heiglnstadt [sic] on 10th October 1802 thus I take leave of you – and sadly too – Yes, the fond hope which I brought here with me that at least I might be healed to a certain extent – I now abandon forever, like the leaves in Autumn, fallen and withering on the ground – so is that hope blighted – I leave this place almost as I came – even that high courage – which often inspired me in the beautiful days of summer – it has now vanished. Oh Providence, vouchsafe me at least one single day. of pure joy! For so long now has that inner echo of true joy been denied to me – When, oh when, oh Divine Godhead – shall I once feel it in the Temple of Nature and among mankind. Never? – No, that would be too hard.

[written lengthwise on the left margin]
For my brothers
Carl and [Johann]
to be read and executed
after my death.
Facsimile, published by Hedwig M. von Asow, Vienna 1957.

In 1801, Haydn had performed his last oratorio, *Die Jahreszeiten* (*The Seasons*), and Beethoven had been present at the first performance to witness Haydn's last triumphant success. Beethoven now thought the time had come for him to turn his attention to the oratorio form, and in 1803 Emanuel Schikaneder—the author of *Die Zauberflöte* (*The Magic Flute*)—offered Beethoven a position as 'house composer' at the Theater an der Wien. Beethoven took lodgings there and was particularly glad of the offer because it enabled him to use the theatre as a concert hall. *Christus am Ölberge* (*Christ on the Mount of Olives*) was first performed there on 4 April 1803, and received a somewhat mixed reception. Despite the grandiose finale, and such brilliant pages as the soldiers' chorus, the work was undoubtedly uneven and unlikely to dislodge *The Creation* or *The Seasons*; indeed, in later years, Beethoven said he regretted setting the part of Christ as an operatic *recitativo accompagnato*.

Wiener Zeitung of Wednesday the 23rd, Saturday the 26th and Wednesday the 30th of March 1803:

Notice.

On 4 April Herr Ludwig van Beethoven will perform a new oratorio with music composed by him:

Christ on the Mount of Olives

in the Imperial-Royal privileged Theater an der Wien. The other pieces which will also be performed will be announced on the large posters.

Ferdinand Ries describes the rehearsal of Christ on the Mount of Olives:

The rehearsal began at eight o'clock in the morning. It was a terrible rehearsal and by half-past two everyone was exhausted and more or less dissatisfied. Prince Carl Lichnowsky, who attended the rehearsal from the start, sent out for great hampers of bread and butter, cold meats and wine. In a friendly way he invited everybody to help themselves, which they did even with both hands, so that everyone was once again in a good humour. Then the Prince requested that the oratorio be tried out once more, so that it might come off well in the evening and Beethoven's first work of this kind be presented to the public in a worthy manner. So the rehearsal began again.   WRBN 76.

August von Kotzebue reports on Beethoven's oratorio Christ on the Mount of Olives *in the periodical* Der Freimüthige:

Even the valiant Beethofen [sic], whose oratorio *Christ on the Mount of Olives* was given for the first time in the theatre in the Wiedner-Vorstadt, was not quite happy and was not able, despite the efforts of his numerous admirers, to obtain much applause. Both the symphonies and parts of the oratorio were received with approval, but the whole was too drawn out, too contrived in construction and lacking in expressive relevance, especially in the vocal writing. The text, by F. X. Huber, seemed as casually thrown together as the music. Yet the performance brought Beethofen 1800 gulden, and he has, together with the celebrated Abbé Vogler, obtained an engagement in that theatre. He will compose one opera while Vogler will write three. For this they receive free lodgings as well as ten percent of the receipts for the first ten performances.

TDR II, 386. (The German writer August von Kotzebue not only wrote plays for the Court Theatre in Vienna but for a while was manager of both theatres; he also edited *Der Freimüthige*. Georg Joseph Vogler [1749–1814] was a composer and famous teacher.)

From the Diary of Joseph Carl Rosenbaum:

Tuesday 5 April 1803. I went to see Fuchs where we talked about the performance of Bethowen's cantata *Christ on the Mount of Olives* today which is sure to come off poorly since Braun is giving the *Creation* in the B[urg] Th[eatre] with both orchestras for the benefit of poor theatre folk.

Wednesday the 6th . . . I spoke to Willmann at the Lusthaus about Bethowen's concert. He praised it, although I heard the opposite opinion from everyone else. Eberl told me that in yesterday's concert Bethowen did not come up to the justifiable expectations of the public and that nothing was really worthy of a great master.   HJB V, 107.

61 George Polgreen Augustus Bridgetower, the virtuoso violinist; drawing by Henry Edridge.

62 Rodolphe Kreutzer, violinist and composer; engraving by C. T. Riedel from a drawing by A. P. Vincent, 1809.

Anton Schindler writes about Beethoven's Christ on the Mount of Olives:

The composer agreed with all this, inasmuch as in later years he declared without reserve that it was a 'mistake' to have treated the part of Christ in a modern operatic manner. The fact that the work remained unperformed after its first performance, as well as the unusually drawn-out delay before its appearance in print (about 1810), would indicate that the author was not particularly satisfied with the work and probably made considerable changes in it.

Schindler I, 91.

Among the many virtuosi of one kind or the other passing through Vienna, a particularly interesting man was George Polgreen Bridgetower, the mulatto son of Prince Nicolaus I Esterházy's personal page, August. Beethoven wrote the A Major Violin Sonata, Op. 47, for Bridgetower in 1803, but afterwards they got into a row over a girl and Beethoven dedicated the Sonata to Rodolphe Kreutzer.

Beethoven's dedication to George Polgreen Bridgetower:

Autograph of the 'Kreutzer-Sonata' in A Major, Op. 47:
'Mulattick Sonata. Composed for the mulatto Brischdauer, great lunatick and mulattick composer.★

Betty Matthews, 'George Polgreen Bridgetower', *The Music Review*, February 1968, p. 22.

★ Sonata mulattica. Composta per il Mulatto Brischdauer gran pazzo e compositore mulattico'.

Letter from Beethoven to the publisher Nikolaus Simrock in Bonn:

Vienna, on the 14th
October
1804

My dear and excellent Herr Simrock!

I have awaited for a long time with longing the Sonata which I gave you – but in vain – please be so kind as to write to me what has happened to it – whether you have just taken it to give to the moths for their dinner – or do you want to have a special imperial privilegium issued to you for it? Now that, I should think, could have been arranged a long time ago. Where does that slothful devil, who should drive out this Sonata, hide – you are usually a pretty swift devil; you are well known for that, like Faust who once made a pact with the dark one, and just on account of that you are so beloved by your comrades. Now once more – where does your devil hide – or what kind of a devil is it who is sitting on my Sonata and with whom you cannot come to an understanding? Hurry up then and send me news when I shall see the S[onata] brought out into the light of day. When you let me know the day, I will write a little note to Kreutzer which you will be so kind as to enclose in his copy (inasmuch as you do send copies to Paris or even have them engraved there). This Kreutzer is a good dear fellow who gave me much enjoyment when he was here – his modesty and his natural ways appeal to me much more than all the exterieur or inferieur of most virtuosos. Since the Sonata was written for a competent violinist, the dedication to him is all the more appropriate. Although we correspond (that is, a letter once a year from me) I hope he will know nothing about it. I hear all the time that you are constantly improving your fortunate position and that pleases me very much indeed. Give my greetings to all your family and all those others whom you think would appreciate my greetings. Please give me an early reply.

Beethoven.

Kal 143. Anderson 99. (The letter deals with the 'Kreutzer' Sonata.)

Ferdinand Ries relates his first experience of Beethoven's deafness to Heinrich Friedrich Ludwig Rellstab:

[c. 1804]

One morning in the summer, when Beethoven lived in Baden, I [Ries] arrived to take a lesson. When I entered the house, I heard him improvising in his room. In order not to disturb him, I remained listening at the door and noticed that, strictly speaking, he was not really improvising but that he was rhapsodically going over isolated passages, seemingly casting them now in one way and then in another. After a few moments he rose from the instrument and opened the window. I went in. He greeted me in a very cheerful voice and said: 'We won't have a lesson today. Instead let us take a walk together, the morning is so beautiful.' Beethoven took a particular pleasure in wandering along lonely, often pathless, ways through the forests, valleys and mountains. We set out happily together and soon found ourselves in lonely woods on the beautiful mountain slopes of Baden. I observed that Beethoven was much absorbed in private meditation and that he was humming to himself; I knew from experience that at such moments he was in the most powerful throes of creation and so I took good care not to disturb him but walked along with him in silence. In some isolated phrases which he was humming to himself, I thought I recognized a similarity to what he had been playing in his room. It was evident that he was engaged on a major work. After having walked for about an hour, we sat down to rest in the grass. Suddenly, from the slope on the other side of the valley, the sound of a shawm was heard, whose unexpected melody under the clear blue spring sky, in the deep solitude of the woods, made a remarkable impression on me. Since Beethoven was sitting next to me I could not refrain from calling his attention to it: sunk deep in thought he had heard nothing. He listened, but I observed from his expression that he did not hear the sounds, although they continued. It was then that for the first time I was convinced his hearing was impaired. Previously I had had the same impression; but since in the early stages this condition came and went periodically, as it did even later, I had thought that I was mistaken. This time, however, there was no doubt whatever in my mind about it. The sounds continued so bright and clear that it was not possible to miss even a single note: yet Beethoven heard nothing. In order not to sadden him, I made believe that I too could not hear anything any more. After a while we set out again, the tones accompanying us for a long time on our solitary way through the woods, without Beethoven's taking the least notice of them. The sweet fascination which these tones had exercised on me at first now turned into a profound sadness. Almost without realizing it, I walked along silently, sunk in sad thoughts, at the side of my great master, who, as before, occupied with his own inner meditations, continued to hum indistinguishable phrases and tones, and to sing aloud. When after several hours we returned home, he sat down impatiently at the piano and exclaimed: 'Now I shall play something for you.' With irresistible

fire and mighty force he played the *Allegro* of the great F Minor Sonata.★
The day will forever remain unforgettable to me.

Kerst I, 106 f. Heinrich Friedrich Ludwig Rellstab, *Aus meinem Leben*, Berlin 1861, II,
257. (Rellstab, from Berlin, whose father was a publisher, came to Vienna in 1825.)

This, 1804, is the year of the *Eroica*, the work which, more than any other except
Beethoven's own Ninth, changed the history of the symphony. Its huge size – twice
the length of any Haydn or Mozart symphony – and vast complexity made it more
than problematical for many of Beethoven's contemporaries. Up to now, with
very few exceptions, Beethoven's compositions had been almost unmitigatedly
successful; with the *Eroica*, Beethoven began to move forward faster than many of
his contemporaries could comprehend. Yet even the most difficult of Beethoven's
compositions, such as the last String Quartets, always had their staunch admirers
among what was becoming known as the Beethoven 'clique'. And such an astute
critic as Haydn's biographer, Georg August Griesinger, summed up public opinion
in his usually perspicacious way when writing to the publishers Breitkopf &
Härtel after the first public performance in 1805. Much of the autograph was completed in Döbling. Beethoven originally intended to dedicate the Symphony to
Napoleon but, as the documents show, he became furious when Napoleon crowned
himself Emperor and tore up the dedication; later, Beethoven conceived a furious
dislike of all things French.

   The history of the *Eroica* involves another of Beethoven's patrons: Franz Joseph
Max, Prince von Lobkowitz, for whom Haydn had written the Quartets, Op. 77.
Lobkowitz's private orchestra played the first performances of many Beethoven
compositions in the first fifteen years of the nineteenth century.

Dr Andreas Bertolini tells Otto Jahn in 1852 about the origins of the Eroica:

The first idea for the Eroica Symphony came to Beethoven from Bonaparte's expedition to Egypt; the rumour of Nelson's death in the Battle
of Aboukir occasioned the Funeral March.

Kerst II, 194. (Dr Bertolini was Dr Malfatti's assistant and Beethoven's friend and
medical adviser.)

*Christoph Kuffner tells Music Director Krenn about Beethoven's opinion of
the* Eroica:

Court Councillor Kuffner told Music Director Krenn that he had lived
with Beethoven in Heiligenstadt and had often gone with him to Nussdorf to eat fish at the inn *Zur Rose*. Once, when Beethoven was in good
humour, Krenn asked which of his symphonies was his favourite, and
he answered pleasantly, 'Eh, Eh, the Eroica.' Krenn, 'I would have
thought the C Minor.' Beethoven, 'No, the Eroica.'

Kerst II, 196. (The poet Christoph Kuffner had been a friend of Beethoven.)

★ Op. 57, 'Appassionata,' begun in 1804 and completed two years later.

From the periodical, Der Freimüthige, *No. 83, 26 April 1805:*

One party, Beethoven's most special friends, contend that this particular symphony [No. 3, *Eroica*] is a masterpiece, that this is exactly the true style for music of the highest type and that if it does not please now it is because the public is not sufficiently cultivated in the arts to comprehend these higher spheres of beauty; but after a couple of thousand years its effect will not be lessened. The other party absolutely denies any artistic merit to this work. They claim that it reveals the symptoms of an evidently unbridled attempt at distinction and peculiarity, but that neither beauty, true sublimity nor power have anywhere been achieved either by means of unusual modulations, by violent transitions or by the juxtaposition of the most heterogeneous elements – when, for example, a Pastorale in the grandest style is developed through violent rents in the basses, by three horns and other similar tricks, a certain, but not desirable, originality can be achieved without much effort. But the creation of something beautiful and sublime, not the production of something merely unusual and fantastic, is the true expression of genius. Beethoven himself, in his own early works, has proven the truth of this statement. The third, very small party stand in the middle. They concede that there are many beautiful things in the symphony, but admit that the continuity often appears to be completely confused and that the endless duration of this longest and perhaps most difficult of all symphonies is tiring even for the expert; for a mere amateur it is unbearable. One wishes that H[err] v[an] B[eethoven] would use his recognized great talent to present us with works similar to his first two Symphonies in C and D, to his agreeable Septet in E flat, the spirited Quintet in D Major [C Major?] and others of his early compositions which will always assure B. a place among the foremost instrumental composers. One fears, however, that if Beethoven continues along this road, he and the public will make a bad journey. Music could easily reach a stage where everyone who has not been vouchsafed a thorough knowledge of the rules and difficulties of the art will derive absolutely no pleasure from it. Overwhelmed by a mass of disconnected and overloaded ideas and by a continuing tumult of all the instruments, the listener would leave the concert hall with only an unpleasant feeling of exhaustion. On that evening, the audience and H. v. Beethoven, who himself conducted, were not mutually pleased with one another. For the audience the Symphony was too difficult, too long and B. himself too rude, for he did not deign to give even a nod to the applauding part of the audience. Beethoven, on the contrary, did not find the applause sufficiently enthusiastic.

TDR II, 459 f.

The fair copy of the score with the dedication to the First Consul of the French Republic, which consisted only of the two words **Napoleon Bonaparte**, was ready to be given to General Bernadotte for transmission to Paris, when the news was received in Vienna that Napoleon Bonaparte had had himself proclaimed Emperor of the French. The news reached the composer through Prince Lichnowsky and Ferdinand Ries. No sooner had he heard the news than he seized the score, tore off the title-page and threw it on the floor, all the while cursing the new Emperor of the French as the 'new tyrant'. Considering the distance which, at that time, separated the Austrian and French capitals it may be readily imagined that Napoleon's accession to the throne caused all the more surprise in Vienna, where there had been no word of the impending plebiscite, for according to the latest assurance that Act of State went into effect with the same hastiness as took place forty-eight years later.

The righteous anger of our democratic composer did not calm down for a very long time, and then not without the persuasiveness of his friends. Finally his aroused passion gave way to a more reasoned contemplation of the recent event. He consented that this new work should be published under the title of **Sinfonia Eroica** with a sub-heading **Per festeggiare il sovvenire d'un gran' uomo**. Nevertheless, the publication occurred fully two years after the foregoing events.

But as for his admiration of Napoleon, it was ended for all time; it turned into a violent hatred. Only after the tragic death of the Emperor in St Helena could Beethoven forgive him. Is it not perhaps possible to discern in this stubbornness a trait handed down as an inheritance from his Netherlands' ancestry? In fact, there was no lack of sarcastic remarks regarding this world-shaking event. For example he said that he had

63 Napoleon Bonaparte; oil portrait by Anne Louis Girodet-Troison. Once Beethoven's model of democratic principles, Napoleon lost his sympathy when he crowned himself Emperor.

93

composed the proper music for this catastrophe – meaning the Funeral March in the **Eroica**. Referring later to this movement he went even further, stating that the middle motive in **C Major** symbolized a new star of hope in the adverse fortunes of Napoleon (the reappearance on the political scene in 1815), and the powerful decision of the great hero's spirit to withstand the fates until the moment of resignation, when the hero sinks down and allows himself to be buried like any mortal.

In January [1805] the **Sinfonia Eroica** received its first performance, following a performance of the one in **C Major**. Regarding this new creation, whose intended dedication had aroused the interest of the public, the *Allg. Mus. Ztg.* Jahrg. VII, 321, gave the following verdict:

'This long, extremely difficult composition is actually a very long drawn-out, daring and wild fantasy. There is no lack of striking and beautiful passages in which one must recognize the energetic and talented spirit of their creator; but very often it seems to lose itself in anarchy. . . . The reviewer undoubtedly belongs to Beethoven's most sincere admirers, but he must admit to finding too much that is shrill and bizarre, whereby an overall view is made difficult and any sense of unity is almost completely absent.'
Schindler I, 107 ff.

Countess Lulu von Thürheim writes about Prince von Lobkowitz:

From morning to night he was occupied with music and squandered a large fortune in order to maintain the most outstanding musicians and singers in the city and on his country estates. In his castle at Eisenberg the door was open to artists and the dinner table was laid uninterruptedly. There the Prince kept up a truly royal state and even today in the neighbourhood they still tell about his magnificent entertainments. He himself composed several operas and, although he walked with a crutch, he took an active part in the performances. Even though he was himself a spendthrift, his purse was open to all and sundry who called on him for help. He died quite young and left his seven small children nothing but a load of debts, the larger part of which it was not possible to pay off. Since his wife, born a Princess Schwarzenberg, had pre-deceased him, her brother Joseph Schwarzenberg took charge of all these orphaned children. . . . Ten years later Karl Schwarzenberg, who had led the allied armies as Supreme Commander, requested as a reward for his services to his fatherland and to the whole of Europe, the payment of his late brother-in-law's debts. The somewhat less generous Emperor took

him at his word, since he could hardly refuse a reward after such brilliant successes, but in order to whittle down the reward, acceded to his request insofar as he lent a considerable sum of money to the trustee of the young Prince Lobkowitz at a low rate of interest. In this manner the Lobkowitz fortunes were enabled to recover during the long trusteeship and the present Prince, who is more economical but less generous than his father, once again enjoys a large fortune.

Countess Lulu von Thürheim, *Mein Leben*, ed. René van Rhyn, Zurich 1923 (4 vols), I, 137f.

Ferdinand Ries writes about the Eroica:

In 1803 Beethoven composed his third symphony (now known as the *Sinfonia eroica*) in Heiligenstadt, a village about one and a half hours from Vienna. When he was composing, Beethoven often had some particular object in mind although he frequently laughed and roared over musical painting, particularly in its more trumpery aspects. Sometimes even *The Creation* and *The Seasons* suffered thereby; not that Beethoven would belittle Haydn's greater qualities, in fact he meted out the highest praise on many choruses and other things of Haydn. In this symphony Beethoven had Buonaparte in mind, but this was when he was First Consul. At that time Beethoven held him in the very highest esteem and compared him with the greatest of the Roman Consuls. Not only I myself but several of his closest friends had seen this symphony, already in full score, lying on his table; at the head of the title page was the word 'Buonaparte' and quite at the foot was written 'Luigi van Beethoven', but no other word. Whether or how the intervening gap was to be filled out I do not know. I was the first person who brought him the news that Buonaparte had declared himself Emperor. Thereupon he flew into a rage and cried out, 'He too is nothing but an ordinary man! Now he will trample underfoot all the Rights of Man and only indulge his ambition: he will now set himself on high, like all the others, and become a tyrant!' Beethoven went to the table, siezed the title-page from the top, tore it up completely and threw it on the floor. The first page was written out anew and it was now that the symphony received the title *Sinfonia eroica*. Later Prince Lobkowitz bought this composition from Beethoven for his own use for a few years and it was given in his palace several times. Here it once happened that Beethoven, who was himself conducting, in the second part of the first Allegro where it goes on for so long in half-notes on the off-beat, threw the orchestra out to such an extent that they had to start again from the beginning. In the same Allegro Beethoven has a wicked trick for the horn; a few bars before the theme comes in again

64, 65 Franz Joseph Max, Prince von Lobkowitz, and his wife, Caroline; anonymous oil portraits copied from paintings by A. F. Oelenhainz.

66 The Lobkowitz Palace in Vienna; coloured engraving by V. Reim. Prince Lobkowitz was an excellent violinist and maintained a private orchestra which gave the first performance of the 'Eroica' Symphony.

complete, Beethoven lets the horn indicate the theme where the two violins still play the chord of the second. For someone who is not familiar with the score this always gives the impression that the horn player has counted wrong and come in at the wrong place. During the first rehearsal of this symphony, which went appallingly, the horn-player, however, came in correctly. I was standing next to Beethoven and, thinking it was wrong, I said, 'That damned horn player! Can't he count properly? It sounds infamously wrong!' I think I nearly had my ears boxed – Beethoven did not forgive me for a long time.   WRBN 77 ff.

Letter from Georg August Griesinger to Breitkopf und Härtel:

[13 February 1805]
. . . This much I can, however, assure you; that the Symphony has been heard at Academies at Prince Lobkowitz's and at an active music-lover's named Wirth, with unusual applause. That it is a work of genius, I hear from both admirers and detractors of Beethoven. Some people say that there is more in it than in Haydn and Mozart, that the Symphony-Poem has been brought to new heights! Those who are against it find that the whole lacks rounding out; they disapprove of the piling up of colossal ideas. . . .

Der Bär – Year Book of Breitkopf und Härtel for the year 1927. Wilhelm Hitzig, *Aus den Briefen Griesingers an Breitkopf und Härtel entnommene Notizen über Beethoven,* p. 32.

Among Beethoven's most intimate friends were the young members of the Brunsvik family. With Franz Count von Brunsvik Beethoven was actually so intimate that they used the 'Du' form when addressing each other. Countess Therese was a faithful friend to Beethoven throughout her life, and with Countess Josephine, Beethoven's friendship gradually grew into something much deeper; he wanted very much to marry her in the winter of 1805, and it was probably only his rather insecure economic situation that prevented her from agreeing to the match. The Brunsviks, and also Count Joseph Deym (Josephine's husband who died in 1804), appear again and again throughout Beethoven's life. Giulietta, Countess Guicciardi, was also a cousin of the young Brunsviks.

From the Memoirs of Therese von Brunsvik:

I was extremely weak and delicate, with a deformed spinal column. At the age of three this was combined with the so-called English disease. The nervous system in particular remained delicate.
. . . When we were in Vienna for those 18 remarkable days, my mother wished to obtain for her two daughters, Therese and Josephine, the priceless musical instruction of Beethoven. As Adalbert Rosti, a school-friend of my brother assured us, Beethoven could not be induced to

accept a simple invitation. However, if Her Excellency would take the trouble to climb the three flights of the spiral staircase in St Peter's Square and pay a call on him, he [Rosti] would vouch for success. And so it turned out. Taking my Beethoven Sonata with Violin and Violoncello accompaniment under my arm like a girl going to school, we went in. The immortal and adored Louis van Beethoven was most friendly and as courteous as he knew how to be. After a little small talk *de part et d'autre* he sat me down at his out-of-tune piano and I started right in, singing the violin and violoncello accompaniment, and managed to play quite well. This delighted him to such an extent that he promised to come daily to the Hotel *Zum Erherzog Carl* – at that time called *Goldene Greifen*. This was the last year of the previous century, in May. He came regularly and moreover often stayed, instead of an hour, from 12 o'clock until 4 or 5 o'clock and did not tire of holding down and bending my fingers, which I had been taught to raise and hold flat. This noble man must have been very pleased; for during all the sixteen days he did not miss a single one. . . .

TDR II, 304, and '*Beethoven*', *dreizehn unbekannte Briefe an Josephine Gräfin Deym geb. v. Brunsvik*, ed. Joseph Schmidt-Görg. Bonn 1957, p. 7.

Letter from Therese von Brunsvik to her sister Josephine von Deym, on 2 February 1811:

I too have received through Franz a memento of our noble Beethoven

67 Therese Countess von Brunsvik, who took piano lessons with Beethoven and developed an 'intimate and warm-hearted friendship' for him; oil portrait by J. B. Lampi the Elder.

68 Franz Count von Brunsvik, to whom Beethoven dedicated his Piano Sonata, Op. 57 ('Appassionata'); oil portrait by H. Thugut.

69 Josephine Countess von Brunsvik, sister of Therese; anonymous oil portrait.

which gives me pleasure. I do not mean his Sonatas, which are very beautiful, but a short note which I shall copy for you immediately.

'Even without intention, the better people think of one another, and this is also the case between you and me, worthy and honoured Therese. I am still indebted to you and must express my heartfelt thanks for your beautiful picture. And if I accuse myself as a debtor, so must I soon appear in the guise of a beggar inasmuch as I beg of you, when you feel the spirit of painting within you, to draw anew that small drawing, which I was so unlucky as to lose. It was an eagle looking at the sun; I cannot forget it. But I pray you, do not believe that I think of myself in that guise, although such thoughts have been ascribed to me. But many people like to look upon heroic scenes and derive pleasure from them, without any feeling of kinship with them. Farewell, worthy Therese, and think sometimes about your truly devoted friend

Beethoven.'

Therese von Brunsvik to her sister on 23 February 1811:

What I beg of you, beloved Josephine, is that picture which you could bring to life once again better than anyone. . . .

We await no other answer to our supreme command than Yes/Yes/Yes!/ six times as fast as lightning – otherwise our wrath will reach you as far as Ofen.

The other news regarding the return journey, you will receive soon.

TDR III, 270 f. Anderson 295.

70 Galerie Müller in the Rotenturmstrasse, Vienna, which was owned and run by Joseph Count Deym von Střítěž, Josephine von Brunsvik's first husband; coloured etching by Maria Geissler, *c.* 1800.

From the diary of Joseph Carl Rosenbaum:

Monday 18 [April 1803] . . . After 7 o'clock Stessel and I went to the Müller Art Gallery which was lit up by Winger's thermo lamps. . . . He [Count Deym, the owner of the gallery] assured me that 22 lamps were burning in the gallery, and led me to the furnace from which the light is fed by means of pipes to all the rooms. From 6 o'clock to 10 o'clock in the evening this lighting consumes 1 Florin 30 Kreutzer worth of wood, or thereabouts.

HJB V, 108.

Letter from Beethoven to Countess Josephine von Deym:

[Winter 1805]

. . . Yes, it is true that I am not as active as I should have been – but an inner unhappiness has for a long time robbed me of my usual buoyancy, ever since my feelings of love for you, desirable J., began to spring up within me, and this increased further. When we are once more together undisturbed, then you shall be told all about my real suffering and of the struggle which has gone on within me for some time between life and death. A fact which for a long time made me doubt whether there can be any happiness in life on this earth – now it is not half as desperate. I have won your heart. Oh, I know for certain what this will mean to me; my activity will increase once again and – and this I promise you by all I hold highest and most precious, in a short time I will be there, worthier of myself and of yourself. Oh, if only you would be willing to establish my happiness through your love – to increase it. Oh beloved J. it is not a desire for the opposite sex which draws me to you, No, you, your whole self with all your characteristics, have fettered all my feelings, my entire sensitivity, to you. When I came to you I had made the firmest decision not to allow even the tiniest spark of love to light up within me. You overwhelmed me, whether you did it willingly or unwillingly? – That question J. could surely answer for me some day. Oh Heavens, what more could I not tell you – how I think of you – what I feel for you – but how weak, how poor in spirit is this language – at least mine.

For a long, long time may our love last. It is noble – based so much on mutual respect and friendship – indeed the very similarities in so many things – in thinking and in feeling. Oh let me hope that your heart will long beat for me. Mine can only cease beating for you when it no longer beats at all – beloved J. keep well. But I also hope that you may be a little happy through me. Otherwise I would be – selfish.

'Beethoven', dreizehn unbekannte Briefe . . ., op. cit., p. 17 f.

Draft of a letter from Countess von Deym to Beethoven, presumably written in the winter of 1804 or 1805:

The closer association with you, my dear Beethoven, during these winter months left impressions in my innermost self which neither time – nor any other circumstances – will ever destroy. Whether you are happy or unhappy? Would you say to yourself – also – whether you – in this regard, through control – or by giving free rein – would lessen or increase your feelings.

My own spirit which, in any case, was enthusiastic for you even before I knew you, received nourishment from your inclination. A feeling which lies deep within my heart and is not capable of expression, made me love you. Before I met you your music made me enthusiastic for you – the goodness of your character, your inclination towards me increased my enthusiasm – this prerogative which you granted me, the pleasure of being with you, could have been the greatest jewel of my life if you loved me less sensually. Because I cannot satisfy this sensual love you are

71 Korompa Castle, the country seat of the Brunsvik family, where Beethoven was often a guest; anonymous oil painting.

angry with me – I would have to destroy sacred bonds if I were to give heed to your desires. Believe me – that the fulfilment of my duties causes me the greatest suffering – and that surely the motives which guide my conduct are noble. *Ibid.*, p. 24 f.

From the diary of Therese von Brunsvik:

[4 February 1846]
... Beethoven! It seems like a dream that he was the friend, the intimate of our house – a stupendous spirit! Why did not my sister J., as the widow Deym, accept him as her husband? She would have been happier than she was with St[ackelberg]. Maternal love caused her to forego her own happiness.

[12 July 1817]
Josephine must suffer remorse on account of Luigi's sorrow – his wife! What could she not have made of this Hero! *Ibid.*, pp. 27, 36.

Vienna's fashionable society included, as we have seen, many pianists so expert that they could be, and indeed were, considered professional. One of the most brilliant was Dorothea Baroness von Ertmann, the wife of an Austrian army officer. Baroness Dorothea became a specialist in performing Beethoven's piano music, and theirs was an intimate friendship which at one point may actually have become something more: the latest research indicates that, of all the known candidates, Baroness Dorothea seems most likely to have been the recipient of the famous letters to the 'immortal beloved'. Her piano-playing was greatly admired by her contemporaries, and there is also an interesting account by Felix Mendelssohn-Bartholdy of her life in Milan after Beethoven's death. Whether or not Baroness von Ertmann really is the 'immortal beloved' it is clear that Beethoven was always very much attracted by pretty women, and we have a sympathetic description of Beethoven's love affairs by Ferdinand Ries. Some of these fashionable ladies even wanted to borrow Beethoven's portrait from him while they were staying in Vienna, as we know from a letter Beethoven wrote to the painter Joseph Willibrord Mähler.

Johann Friedrich Reichardt writes about Baroness von Ertmann:

Vienna, 7 February 1809

As it happens, there also lives in this Bürgerspital a great music lover and connoisseur, and a great friend and admirer of Beethoven, Herr von Zmeskal. He is also a good violoncello player. A new quartet has been established in his apartments on Sunday mornings, which played together for the first time last Sunday. After a difficult quintet by Beethoven had been performed well, we had the good fortune to hear a great Fantasia by Beethoven [Sonata Op. 27, No. 2] played by Frau von Ertmann (wife of Major von Ertmann), with such great power, spirit and perfection that it left us all enchanted. It is not possible to hear anything more perfect on this perfect instrument. It was a beautiful Streicher Fortepiano which was made to sound like an entire orchestra. . . . The previous evening I had already had the fortune to hear Frau von Ertmann at a large reception at her brother-in-law's. But this gathering was more an occasion for the dancing which was to follow and which the numerous handsome young people awaited with impatience. So she purposely chose only agreeable and short pieces in order to satisfy the curiosity of the large company. But she played even those pieces with a precision and elegance which reveal a great mastery. But in that marvellous Fantasia which seemed to me to be in C sharp minor, she developed the same qualities to the fullest extent and to an astounding degree. I do not recall ever having heard anything greater or more consummate. This great artistic talent is not, however, a native of this country. Frau von Ertmann was born a Graumann from Frankfurt-am-Main, but has lived now for several years in this artistic country and has derived her greatest benefit from her closeness to Beethoven.   Reichardt I, 309 ff.   103

72 Dorothea Baroness von Ertmann; miniature on ivory by J. D. Oechs. Baroness Ertmann was an excellent pianist and one of the very greatest interpreters of Beethoven's sonatas. He dedicated to his 'Dorothea Cäcilia' the Piano Sonata in A, Op. 101.

Felix Mendelssohn-Bartholdy writes about Baroness von Ertmann:

Milan, 14 July 1831

She [Baroness von Ertmann] told me that when she lost her last child, Beethoven was at first unable to come to her house any more. Finally he invited her to come to him, and when she came he sat at the piano and merely said: 'We will now converse in music,' and played for over an hour and, as she expressed it, 'He said everything to me, and also finally gave me consolation.'

TDR II, 415. (The famous composer, in the course of his journey to Italy, had called on the Baroness, whose husband, now a General, was stationed in Milan, and admired her piano-playing.)

Antonie von Arneth speaks of Baroness von Ertmann to Alexander Wheelock Thayer on 25 December 1864:

After the funeral of her [Baroness Ertmann's] only child she could not find tears. . . . General Ertmann brought her to Beethoven. The Master spoke no words but played for her until she began to sob, so her sorrow found an outlet and comfort.

TDR III, 583. (Antonie Adamberger, the popular Viennese actress, later married Joseph von Arneth. She played the part of Klärchen in Goethe's *Egmont*, to which Beethoven composed the music.)

Anton Schindler writes about the Baroness von Ertmann:

Without Frau von Ertmann, Beethoven's piano music would have vanished much sooner from the repertoire in Vienna. For it was this lady, at once tall, beautiful and with refined taste, who from purely altruistic motives entertained a love of higher things and who opposed the emergence of a new approach towards composition and playing fostered by Hummel and his neophytes. Beethoven thus had double reason to honour her as a priestess of music: he used to call her his 'Dorothea-Cecilia'. Another key to her success in reproducing music at the highest level was that Frau von Ertmann, characteristically, never placed anything on her music stand that did not suit her personality.
Schindler I, 242.

Letter from Beethoven to Dorothea von Ertmann:

Vienna, 23 February 1816
[correctly 1817]

My dear, treasured Dorothea-Cecilia!
   You must often have misjudged me in cases when I have appeared to oppose you. Much of this was due to circumstances, especially in the earlier days, when <u>my idiom was less</u> recognized than it is now. You know the protestations of the unbidden Apostles who made shift with means quite different from the Holy Gospel – I would not wish to be counted among their number – Receive now what has often been promised to you★ and what you may take as a token of my admiration for both your artistic talent and your own person. . . . I hope to hear soon from you how the Muses flourish in Sankt Pölten★★ and whether you still have esteem for your

admirer and friend
L. v. Beethoven.

All best wishes to your worthy <u>husband and consort</u>.
TDR IV, 18. Anderson 764.

Franz Grillparzer describes Beethoven's appearance:

At that time he was still slim, dark and, in contrast to his later habits, very elegantly dressed. He wore glasses, which I noticed particularly, because in later times he no longer made use of this aid for short-sightedness.
FRBS I, 27.

★ Evidently a reference to the Sonata in A Major, Op. 101 (*Hammerklavier*).
★★ At that time Baron von Ertmann's regiment was stationed in Sankt Pölten in Lower Austria.

The invasion of Vienna by Napoleon's troops in 1805 coincided, most unfortunately, with the première of Beethoven's only opera, *Fidelio*. To find a good libretto for a German opera had always been a serious problem for composers. Both Mozart's *Abduction from the Seraglio* and *The Magic Flute* are markedly inferior to the Da Ponte libretti (of which, incidentally, Beethoven did not approve – he thought the subjects frivolous); and Beethoven had very definite ideas concerning the ethic and moral standards of the libretti suitable in his eyes for an operatic subject. After the disastrous reception in 1805, Beethoven revised the opera in 1806, when it was much more successful; he again worked over the whole opera for the next performance in 1814, and after that *Fidelio* was an unqualified success. Again, many people, such as Joseph Carl Rosenbaum, found that the music was 'pretty, artistic and difficult'; but the public gradually caught up with Beethoven's unfettered fantasy.

Louis Schlösser writes about the first performance of Fidelio :

Napoleon's headquarters were [in 1805] in Schönbrunn; the French military filled the rooms at the Opera House. Was it imaginable that the ethical purity and chaste beauty of a work, whose language they could not even understand, could awaken a sympathetic echo from guests who were accustomed to more frivolous fare?

Kerst II, 4. (Kapellmeister Schlösser came in 1822 to Vienna, and visited Beethoven. He wrote his Memoirs for the periodical *Hallelujah*, No. 20/21, 4th year, 1885.)

From the Diary of Joseph Carl Rosenbaum :

[20 November 1805]

At the [Theater] an der Wien the first performance of Beethowen's Grand Opera *Fidelio* or *Conjugal Love* in 3 Acts; freely [adapted] from the French by Jos. Sonnleithner. . . . In the evening I went to the Th. W. to hear Louis Beth.'s opera. . . . The opera contains pretty, artistic and difficult music, a boring, not very interesting book. It was not a success, and the theatre was empty.

HJB V, 129.

Georg Friedrich Treitschke reports on Fidelio :

From the distance the thunder of war was rolling towards Vienna and this robbed audiences of the serenity necessary for the enjoyment of a work of art. Particularly in view of this situation, everything possible was done to enliven the sparsely filled house. *Fidelio* was thought to be a trump card, and so the opera opened on 20 November under stars which were in no way propitious. Only the women's parts could be satisfactorily cast with Mlles Milder and Müller; the men left all the more to be desired.

TDR II, 481. (Georg Friedrich Treitschke, a libretto writer and stage director, later revised the text of *Fidelio* for Beethoven.)

Criticism of Beethoven's Fidelio *(by August von Kotzebue?):*

The entry of the French into Vienna was an experience to which, at first, the Viennese could not become accustomed, and for a few weeks a most unusual silence reigned. The Court, the courtiers and most of the great landowners had left; instead of the usual ceaseless rattle of coaches lumbering through the streets, one rarely heard so much as a simple cart creeping by. The streets were peopled mainly with French soldiers who, on the whole, maintained good discipline. In the city itself almost exclusively officers were quartered; the other ranks were billeted in the outskirts. It was only natural that people gave little thought to entertainment; the difficulty of obtaining provisions was very great, and the fear of possible collisions and unpleasant encounters kept the majority of men and women at home. The theatres were also quite empty at the beginning, and only after a while did the French begin to attend them; and it is still they who comprise the greater majority of the spectators.

Recently little of importance has been given. A new opera by Beethoven, *Fidelio*, or *Conjugal Love*, did not find favour. It was performed only a few times, and immediately following the first performance it played to quite empty houses. Moreover, the music falls far below the expectations to which connoisseurs and music-lovers consider themselves entitled. The melodies and characterization, in spite of many felicities, lack that happy, striking, overwhelming expression of passion which, in Mozart's and Cherubini's works, moves us so irresistibly. The music has some attractive passages but it is very far from being a perfect or even a successful work. The text, translated by Sonnleithner, consists of one of those liberation stories which have come into fashion since Cherubini's *Deux Journées*.

TDR II, 488 f. *Der Freimüthige*, 26 December 1805.

Joseph August Röckl speaks about the revision of Fidelio*:*

It was December 1805, the Oper an der Wien and both Court Theatres were at that time under the management of the *intendant* Baron Braun, the Court banker. Herr Meyer, Mozart's brother-in-law and the stage manager of the Oper an der Wien came to me and invited me to an evening party at the palace of Prince Carl Lichnowsky, the great protector of Beethoven. *Fidelio* had been performed a month previously at the Theater an der Wien, unfortunately just after the French military occupation when the Inner City was cut off from the suburbs.

The whole theatre was filled with Frenchmen, and only a few of Beethoven's friends ventured out to hear the opera. These friends were gathered at Prince Lichnowsky's in order to persuade Beethoven to give his consent to the changes which had to be made in the opera in order to overcome the heaviness of the first act. The necessity for these improvements had already been recognized and determined between them. Meyer had prepared me for the impending storm which would burst when Beethoven was told that three entire numbers would have to be cut from the first act.

The company consisted of Prince Lichnowsky and the Princess his wife, Beethoven and his brother Caspar, [Stephan] von Breuning, [Heinrich] von Collin the poet, the actor Lange (another brother-in-law of Mozart's), Treitschke, Clement the conductor of the orchestra, Meyer and myself. Whether Kapellmeister v. Seyfried was present or not I can no longer remember for certain, although I think he was.

I had come to Vienna only a short time before, and it was here that I met Beethoven for the first time. Since the whole opera had to be gone through, we went to work immediately. Princess Lichnowsky played the piano from the large orchestra score and Clement, who sat in a corner of the room, accompanied the whole opera from memory on his violin,. playing all the solos of the various instruments. Since Clement's uncanny memory was a matter of common knowledge, no one but myself was in the least astonished at this feat. Meyer and I made ourselves useful by singing, to the best of our abilities, he (a bass) the lower and I in the higher parts of the opera. Although Beethoven's friends were fully prepared for the coming battle they had never before seen him in *such* a fury. Without the pleas and tears of the very delicate and gentle Princess, who was a second mother to Beethoven, and recognized as such by him, his united friends would probably have had difficulty achieving any success whatever in this undertaking, which seemed to them besides a very doubtful proposition. But after their united efforts, which lasted from seven o'clock to after one at night, the sacrifice of three numbers was accepted. And worn out, hungry and thirsty, as we prepared to restore ourselves with a lavish supper, no one was in a happier or merrier mood than Beethoven. If I had seen him first in his wrath, now I saw him in a good humour. When he saw me sitting opposite him busy dealing with a French dish, he asked what I was eating. I answered that I did not know. Thereupon he roared out in his leonine voice, 'He eats like a wolf, without knowing what! Ha! Ha! Ha!'

TDR II, 492 ff.
(Joseph August Röckl sang Florestan in *Fidelio*. He related his experience to Alexander W. Thayer on 26 February 1861.)

Letter from Joseph Sonnleithner to State Councillor von Stahl on 3 October 1805:

You will eternally oblige Her Majesty the Empress, the public which is noticeably abandoning the theatre because it cannot be served according to its wishes and has waited for a long time for an opera by Beethoven, and the theatre whose duty is always to fulfil as far as possible the desires of the high authorities.

It is true that a Minister abuses his powers, but only to indulge in a private revenge – in Spain – in the 16th century – moreover he is punished, punished by the Court and he is confronted with the heroism of womanly virtue. . . .

Carl Glossy, *Zur Geschichte der Theater Wiens*, Vienna 1915, I, 83. (On 5 October the performance was authorized by the censors 'after a few changes in the more problematical sections.')

Baron de Trémont on Beethoven's reactions to Napoleon:

At the Imperial Court in Vienna he was regarded as a republican. Far from patronizing him, the Court never attended the performance of even a single one of his compositions. Napoleon had been his hero as long as he remained First Consul of the Republic. After the battle of Marengo he worked on his hero-symphony (*Eroica*) with the intention of dedicating it to him [Napoleon]. The symphony was completed in 1802 when it began to be rumoured that Napoleon wished to be crowned and then to subject Germany to his rule. Beethoven tore up his dedication and transferred his hatred to the French nation which had bowed beneath the yoke. Nevertheless, the greatness of Napoleon interested him a great deal and he often talked about it with me. In spite of his poor opinion of Napoleon, I realized that he admired Bonaparte for having risen so high from such humble origins. This appealed to his democratic ideas. One day he said to me 'Would I be obliged to pay homage to your Emperor if I came to Paris?' I assured him that it would not be necessary for him to do so, so long as he was not commanded. 'And do you think that I would be summoned?' 'I have no doubt you would be if Napoleon knew who you were, but you have heard from Cherubini how little he understands about music.'

This question led me to think that, in spite of his convictions, it would have flattered him if he had been decorated by Napoleon. Human pride bows down in the face of flattery.

Kerst I, 139 f. *Mercure Musical*, 1906, No. 9. (Baron de Trémont, a French official, was in Vienna during the French occupation and visited Beethoven.)

73 Rudolph von Habsburg, Cardinal and Archbishop of Olmütz; oil portrait by J. B. Lampi the Elder, 1805. Archduke Rudolph became Beethoven's pupil in the winter of 1803–04 and a friendship developed between them.

Beethoven's opinion of Napoleon:

Even with that Bastard I made a mistake.

Kerst II, 192.

Ferdinand Ries discusses Beethoven's waywardness:

Etiquette and all that goes with it was something that Beethoven never learned and never wanted to learn; thus his behaviour often caused great embarrassment to the *suite* of the Archduke Rudolph when Beethoven first attended him. They attempted to force him to learn what formalities he had to observe. But this he found insupportable. He did, however, promise to improve, but – that was as far as it went. Finally one day he burst in on the Archduke in a state of exasperation because he was again being, as he put it, tutored. He declared outright that he most certainly had all possible respect for the Archduke's person, but that the stringent instructions and regulations which were being imparted to him every day did not concern him. The Archduke laughed pleasantly over this occurrence and gave orders that Beethoven should be allowed to go his own way without hindrance: that was the way he was.

Kerst I, 95 f.

Letter from Xaver Schnyder von Wartensee to Nägeli in Zurich, 17 December 1811:

I was extremely well received by Beethoven and already have been several times to see him. He is a most unusual man. Great thoughts float through his mind which he can only express through music. Words are not at his command. His whole culture is very neglected and, apart from his art, he is rough but honest and without pretensions. He says straight out what is on his mind. In his youth, and even now, he has had to struggle with disappointments. This has made him suspicious and grim. He rails against Vienna and would like to leave. 'From the Emperor down to the last shoe polisher,' he says, 'the Viennese are all a worthless lot.' I asked him if he took pupils. No, he answered, that was tiresome work. He only has one who gives him a lot of trouble and whom he would be glad to be rid of, if only he could. 'Who is he, then,' I asked. 'The Archduke Rudolph.'

Kerst I, 166. (Schnyder, a Swiss composer, came to Vienna in 1811.)

From the Diary of Fanny Giannastasio del Rio:

At that time, Beethoven gave lessons to the brother of the Emperor Francis, the Archduke Rudolph. I once asked him if he played well. 'When he feels strong enough,' was the answer, given with a smile. He also once told me laughingly that he raps him on the fingers, and once when His Highness wanted to put him back in his place, Beethoven, to indicate his justification, pointed with his finger to a certain line of a poet – it was Goethe, if I am not mistaken.

Kerst I, 215 f. (Fanny Giannastasio's father kept a school in Vienna attended by Beethoven's nephew Carl.)

Louis Schlösser reminisces about Beethoven's relations with the aristocracy:

After he [Beethoven] had drawn his hand across his forehead he replied, 'In my earlier years I had made up my mind to leave Vienna; there were determining reasons which had nothing to do with my profession. Then there were also requests for me from abroad, namely from England and from Kassel, which would have assured me a much higher income, and this would have carried much weight in my situation. When my Imperial patron and pupil, the Archduke Rudolph, heard of my decision he was fearfully upset. "No, No," he cried out, "that must never happen! You shall never leave the place made sacred before you by Mozart and Haydn! Where in the world will you find a second Vienna? I will speak to my brother the Emperor Francis, I will speak to Esterházy, to Liechtenstein, to Palffy, Lobkowitz, Karoly, to all the Princes, so that they may guarantee you a permanent subsidy sufficient to relieve you of all concern for your future existence."'

Kerst II, 11 f. (For Schlösser, see p. 106. Palffy probably Prince Joseph Franz. Karoly probably Count Joseph Karoly von Nagy-Karoly.)

One of Beethoven's most important patrons was Andreas Cyrillovich Prince Razumovsky, Russian Ambassador to the Austrian Court, for whom he wrote his famous 'Razumovsky' Quartets, Op. 59. The success of these great and revolutionary String Quartets induced the Prince to form a regular quartet.

Baroness du Montet describes Prince Razumovsky:

I found the Prince aged and depressed. His extravagant magnificence has ruined him. . . . During the Congress of Vienna, when the Emperor of Austria was discussing the prince with the Tsar Alexander, he called him 'King of one of his suburbs'. . . . He is a great gentleman who commands respect and is generally most amiable. His presence and appearance are imperious; he radiates pride in all things; pride in his birth, his rank and his honour . . . in his bearing, in his speech . . . in short he is proud in all things. . . . Sometimes he is downright haughty. . . . This nobleman was afflicted a few years before his death with the decay of his mental and physical faculties.

Du Montet 150 f.

Anton Schindler writes about the Razumovsky Quartet:

Count Razumovsky was also a practising musician and, to sum him up appropriately in a few words, the chief upholder of the Haydn tradition in instrumental music. Alternating with Prince Lichnowsky, he would also gather the . . . musicians in his palace to perform quartet music, in which he himself played second violin. Soon, however, he decided on another course, which was to give his circle a higher significance: he placed a permanent Quartet under a life-long contract. This was the first and only example of its kind in Austria. Not that other rich art-lovers did not follow this example, establishing permanent quartets in their households; indeed there were several. But none of them did what the Russian Maecenas did, namely to provide these artists with pensions for the rest of their lives.

This model Quartet was composed of the following artists: Schuppanzigh, I Violin; Sina, II Violin; Weiss, Viola; Linke, Violoncello. Under the name 'The Razumovsky Quartet,' they achieved not only a European fame but also a place in the history of music. Nevertheless they never made a single concert tour, a fact in many ways most regrettable, for they would have established standards for the *authentic* performance of classical works, which in our time are sadly lacking.

We have just named Count Razumovsky as the upholder of the Haydn tradition of quartet music. How can this be explained? Very simply: Haydn had revealed to this art-lover [Razumovsky] that *fine* sensitivity necessary to the understanding of many of those particular qualities in his quartets and symphonies which are neither superficial nor conveyed through the usual [musical] symbols. Since these things had eluded other artists, he undertook to acquaint the Count with his hidden intentions so that he might then transmit them to the performing musicians. This fact is of *great* importance in understanding the true qualities of the Razumovsky Quartet, especially as far as Beethoven's quartet-music is concerned; a contributory factor was the youth of the four players, which made it necessary for them to seek instruction from older and more experienced musicians.

Count Razumovsky was one of the first to determine the path of the new musical constellation. Having established his permanent Quartet, he, more than any other of Beethoven's patrons, became closely bound to the composer's future development. For in fact, Razumovsky's Quartet became equally Beethoven's Quartet: it was as if this noble patron had engaged them exclusively for this purpose; they were placed at his complete disposal.

Schindler I, 37 ff.

Schindler on Beethoven and Prince Razumovsky:

There [at Razumovsky's] the master was the object of general attention on the part of all foreigners, for it is in the nature of things that creative genius, particularly when combined with a certain heroic element, attracts the attention of all the nobility. Can we not term it a form of heroism when we consider the composer's struggles against prejudices of every kind: against the traditionalists on account of his art, against the envy, conceit and ill-will of the majority of musicians and, even more than all this, against the loss of the one sense so indispensable in every way to the practice of his art, namely his hearing? And further, when one considers the exalted position which he achieved despite all these struggles? No wonder, then, that everyone made the greatest effort to pay him homage! He was presented by Prince Razumovsky to the assembled monarchs and they expressed their regard for him in the most flattering terms. The Empress of Russia in particular wished to compliment him. The presentation took place in the apartments of the Archduke Rudolph, where he was also greeted by other persons of high standing. It seems that the Archduke wished to share in the triumph of his exalted teacher inasmuch as it was he who had invited the foreign gentlemen to meet Beethoven. In later years the great master recalled, not without emotion, that day in the Imperial *Burg* and in the palace of

74 Autograph page of Beethoven's Fourth Symphony, Op. 60, which was largely composed in 1806 at the Lichnowsky Castle of Grätz.

the Russian prince, and said with a touch of pride that the highest Monarchs had paid court to him, and that he had comported himself in a distinguished manner.   Schindler I, 233 f.

Carl Czerny recalls a performance of Beethoven's Razumovsky Quartet in F Major:

When Schuppanzigh played the Razumovsky Quartet in F for the first time, they laughed and were convinced that Beethoven wanted to play a joke and that this was not the promised quartet at all.   TDR II, 536.

> Beethoven was often a guest at Lichnowsky's summer castle Grätz near Troppau. Most of the Fourth Symphony was written when he was a guest there in the late summer and autumn of 1806. Nearby lived a friend of Lichnowsky's, Franz Count von Oppersdorff, with whom Beethoven was soon on the most friendly terms; he dedicated his Fourth Symphony to Oppersdorff and the surviving correspondence between the two men shows that he intended originally to write the Fifth Symphony for Oppersdorff as well.

75 Grätz Castle near Troppau, Czechoslovakia; detail from painting by F. Amerling. Beethoven was often the guest of Prince Carl Lichnowsky here.

Max Ring speaks of his visit to Grätz Castle:

The old castellan, to whom we had a recommendation from a high official, told us about a number of the famous composer's characteristics. He was firmly convinced that Herr van Beethoven was not quite right in his mind; he would often run, bareheaded, without a hat, around in the great park of the castle hours on end, even if it were raining with lightning and thunder. On other occasions he would sit for whole days shut up in his room without seeing anybody and not speaking a word.

But the most insane behaviour of Herr van Beethoven occurred when the French occupied Grätz after the battle of Austerlitz [1805]. The Prince had aroused the hopes of the French General, a very fine gentleman and a great music-lover, of meeting the celebrated composer and to hear him play on the pianoforte. To this end, a great musical soirée was arranged at the castle and the composer was to play his latest compositions. Beethoven, however, refused although the Prince repeatedly and earnestly requested him to do so. Nevertheless, the Prince still hoped

76 Autograph first page of the Piano
Sonata in F Minor, Op. 57 ('Appassionata'), composed about 1804. The
autograph was completed while Beethoven was at Grätz Castle in the autumn
of 1806.

onata

521.

to persuade the obstinate musician, and invited the French General and other distinguished guests to the intended soirée. On the appointed evening the company was assembled, eagerly awaiting the promised treat, but Beethoven was nowhere to be seen. The Prince sent one attendant after the other, but the musician would not come. Finally the major-domo who had also been sent to Beethoven, brought the news that the artist had left the castle secretly and only a letter to the Prince had been found in his room. In it he explained that he could not play to the enemies of his country. In order to avoid any further pleas or solicitations, Beethoven had fled on foot to the town of Grätz in the cold winter night. This, the old castellan added, was a clear indication of his madness.

Max Ring, *Erinnerungen*, Berlin 1898, p. 24. Kerst I, 124 f. (The physician Max Ring [1817–1901] visited Grätz and spoke to the old castellan who had known Beethoven in the past.)

Dr Anton Weiser on Beethoven's flight from Grätz:

In order to humour them [the French officers], it was promised that after dinner they would have the pleasure of hearing the famous Beethoven, who was then a guest at the castle, play. 'They went to table; one of the French staff officers unhappily asked Beethoven if he also knew the violin.' Weiser, who was also at table, 'saw at once how this outraged the artist . . . Beethoven did not deign to answer his interlocutor.' Weiser could not attend the rest of the dinner since, as Director of the Troppau Hospital, he had to make a professional call there. He heard the rest of the story from Beethoven himself. When the time came for Beethoven to play, he was nowhere to be found. He was looked for. The Prince wanted to persuade him – to cajole him – into playing. No use. An unpleasant, even vulgar, scene took place. Beethoven immediately had his things packed, and hastened, despite the pouring rain, on foot to Troppau, where he spent the night at Weiser's. It was, because of the rain that the Sonata in F Minor Op. 57, the *Appassionata*, which Beethoven was carrying with him was damaged by water. . . . Weiser tells further that the next day it was difficult, without the Prince, to get a passport to return to Vienna. Finally it was procured. Before he left, Beethoven wrote a very self-willed letter to Lichnowsky which is supposed to have read as follows: 'Prince! What you are, you are by circumstance and by birth. What I am, I am through myself. Of princes there have been and will be thousands. Of Beethovens there is only one. . .' Unfortunately, it seems that the march from Grätz to Troppau induced a considerable worsening of Beethoven's deafness. An exaggerated

77 Muzio Clementi; engraving by Edward Scriven from a painting by James Lonsdale, 1819.

tradition even tells us that Beethoven's deafness was the result of the chill.
T. von Frimmel, *Ludwig van Beethoven*, 4th edition, Berlin 1912, p. 44. (Frimmel quotes a report written by Prince Lichnowsky's personal physician.)

> In 1806, Beethoven was persuaded to write his only Violin Concerto, Op. 61, for Franz Clement, leader of the orchestra in the Theater an der Wien. The first performance took place at Clement's benefit concert on 23 December 1806. Later, the famous pianist and composer Muzio Clementi, who was now in the publishing business in London, came to Vienna and made Beethoven's acquaintance. He persuaded Beethoven to rewrite the Violin Concerto for piano, which Beethoven did, adding a fascinating cadenza in the first movement for piano and timpani solo, and dedicating the work to the wife of his old friend Stephan von Breuning, Julie (née von Vering). Clementi's letter to his partner Collard of 22 April 1807 amusingly describes his successful attempts to secure the English rights for various Beethoven compositions, and it is interesting to realize that many of Clementi's Beethoven editions are in fact the first, preceding those on the Continent – for example, the 'Emperor' Concerto, Op. 73.

Ferdinand Ries on Beethoven and Clementi:

When Clementi came to Vienna Beethoven wished to call on him at once; but his brother put it into his head that Clementi should call first. Clementi, although much older, would probably have done this anyway, if some gossip about it had not arisen. So it came about that Clementi was in Vienna for a long time without Beethoven's knowing him except by sight. We often ate mid-day dinner at the same table at the Swan; Clementi with his pupil Klengel (1783–1852), and Beethoven with me. Everyone knew who everyone else was, but neither spoke to the other, or even greeted each other. The two pupils had to follow their masters, probably because each was under the threat of losing his lessons, which for me, at least, would certainly have been irrevocable, since with Beethoven there was never any compromise.

Kerst I, 95.

Letter from Muzio Clementi to the publisher F. W. Collard, London [original English]:

Messrs. Clementi & Co., No. 26 Cheapside, London.
Vienna, April 22d, 1807.

Dear Collard:

By a little management and without committing myself, I have at last made a compleat conquest of that <u>haughty beauty</u>, Beethoven, who first began at public places to grin and coquet with me, which of course I took care not to discourage; then slid into familiar chat, till meeting him by chance one day in the street – 'Where do you lodge?' says he; 'I have not seen you this <u>long</u> while!' – upon which I gave him my address. Two days after I found on my table his card brought by himself, from the maid's description of his lovely form. This will do, thought I. Three days after that he calls again, and finds me at home. Conceive then the mutual ecstasy of such a meeting! I took pretty good care to improve it to our <u>house's</u> advantage, therefore, as soon as decency would allow, after praising very handsomely some of his compositions: 'Are you engaged with any publisher in London?' – 'No' says he. 'Suppose, then, that you prefer <u>me</u>?' – 'With all my heart.' 'Done. What have you ready?' – 'I'll bring you a list.' In short I agreed with him to take in mss. three quartets, a symphony, an overture and a concerto for the violin, which is beautiful, and which, at my request he will adapt for the piano-forte with and without additional keys; and a concerto for the piano-forte, for <u>all</u> which we are to pay him two hundred pounds sterling. The property, however, is only for the British Dominions. To-day sets off a courier for London through Russia, and he will bring over to you two or three of the mentioned articles.

Remember that the violin concerto he will adapt himself and send it as soon as he can. . . .

TDR III, 26.

Among the many Haydn forms which Beethoven intended to stay clear of was the large-scale Mass. Haydn, after he had returned from London, had written six great Masses for the name-day of Princess Hermenegild Esterházy, and now that he was no longer able to compose, Prince Nicolaus II Esterházy asked Beethoven to compose a Mass for Eisenstadt. Through Haydn, Beethoven had long been in touch with the Esterházy family and had dedicated some marches to Princess Hermenegild. The new Mass was ready in 1807 and Beethoven went to Eisenstadt to conduct the first performance. The Mass in C Major, Op. 86, did not find favour, and Prince Nicolaus even went so far as to describe it as 'unbearably ridiculous and detestable', certainly not a tribute to that famous Prince's taste and discernment.

Anton Schindler on Beethoven's religious ideas:

Beethoven was brought up in the Catholic religion. The whole course of his life proves that he was truly religious at heart. The fact that he never discussed religious matters or the dogmas of the various Christian churches, or expressed his opinions about such questions, was one of his peculiar characteristics. It can be stated with relative certainty, however, that his religious views were based far less on faith in the Church than on Deism. Without any specific theory, he acknowledged God in the world, as well as the world in God. The theory for this he found constituted in the whole of nature, and that often-cited book, Christian Sturm's *Betrachtungen der Werke Gottes in der Natur*, as well as the teachings created out of the philosophic systems of the Greek sages, seem to have been the signposts he followed along this path. It would be difficult to assert the opposite if one had observed how he absorbed the significant contents of these writings into his inner life.
Kerst II, 26f. Schindler II, 161.

Letter from Beethoven to Prince Nicolaus Esterházy:

Most Serene and Most Gracious Prince!
Since I have been told that you, my Prince, have inquired after the Mass which you commissioned me to write for you, I allow myself the freedom, most Serene Prince, to inform you that you will receive it at the latest by the 20th of August. This will allow sufficient time to perform it on the name-day of Her Serene Highness the Princess. Unusually advantageous offers were made to me from London, and since, unfortunately, a benefit day in the theatre did not come off, I was obliged to accept them gladly. This delayed the completion of the Mass, although I would have wished to present it to Your Serene Highness in person. Then I was struck down with a head condition which at the beginning prevented me from working at all and still only permits me to work very little. Since people are only too glad to misconstrue everything I do to my disadvantage, I submit for Your S[erene] H[ighness]'s perusal a letter from my physician. May I add that I shall deliver the Mass to you

78 Maria Hermenegild Princess Esterházy, *née* Princess von Liechtenstein; oil portrait by Angelika Kauffmann, 1795. Beethoven's Mass in C, Op. 86, was performed in Eisenstadt in September 1807 to celebrate the Princess's name day.

79 Bergkirche in Eisenstadt, where the Mass was performed with Haydn's orchestra and choir; lithograph by A.L. Jung from a drawing by M. Mayer, 1840.

80 Esterházy Castle in Eisenstadt; coloured steel plate engraving by C. Rorich, from a drawing by L. Rohbock.

with much trepidation, as your S.H. is accustomed to the performance of the inimitable masterpieces of the great Haiden [sic].

Most Serene, Most Gracious Prince,

With respect,

your devoted and humble

Ludwig van Beethoven.

Baden, 26 July [1807].

Anderson 150.

Letter from Dr Schmidt, Beethoven's physician, to Beethoven:

Vienna, 22 July 1807

I was, my dear friend, at first convinced that your headache was caused by gout, and I am still of this opinion since the tooth was extracted. Your pains will be eased but they will not cease in Baden, nor will they in Rodaun, for the *Boreas* is your enemy. Therefore leave Baden, or, if you want to try out Rodaun for 8 days, put a spurge-laurel poultice on your arm straightaway. We can expect nothing more from bleeding, but you will be helped by taking the baths, working little and sleeping, eating well and drinking spirits in moderation.

Greetings and friendship,

Yours, Schmidt

In haste.

Letter from Prince Nicolaus Esterházy to Beethoven:

Most esteemed Herr van Beethoven!

I perceive with much pleasure from your letter from Baden that I can entertain the agreeable hope of receiving a Mass from you before the 20th of this month. This fulfilment will give me all the more pleasure since I expect a great deal from it. Your expressed anxiety about a comparison with Haydn's Masses has only increased the value of your work. I wish you, moreover, the speediest recovery of your complete good health and remain with all esteem

Your most eager,
Nicolaus Prince Esterházy.

Eisenstadt the 9th August 807.

Letter From Prince Esterházy to Countess Henriette von Zielinska [original French]:

. . . Beethoven's Mass is unbearably ridiculous and detestable, and I am not convinced that it can ever be performed properly. I am angry and mortified. Gulistan [an opera by Dalayrac] was well played. This is our news.

Johann Harich, *Beethoven in Eisenstadt*, special supplement from the *Burgenländische Heimatblätter*, Eisenstadt 1959, 21st year, No. 2, pp. 173 ff.

> In 1808, Beethoven had lodgings with a charming and delightful member of the Austro-Hungarian aristocracy, Anna Marie Countess Erdödy, who lived separated from her husband. A gifted pianist, Countess Erdödy gave musical dinner parties, a description of which has come down to us from the distinguished German critic and composer, Johann Friedrich Reichardt.

Johann Friedrich Reichardt writes about Countess Erdödy:

Vienna, 30 November 1808.

I have also sought out and visited the good Beethoven. People pay so little attention to him here that no one could tell me where he lives, and it entailed quite a lot of trouble on my part to locate him. Finally I found him in a large, desolate and lonely apartment. At first he looked as dark as his own lodgings, but soon became more cheerful and even seemed as pleased to see me again as I was heartily glad to see him. He also told me a lot of things which were important for me to know, all in a very frank and agreeable manner. His is a powerful nature, like a cyclops in appearance but at the same time very intimate, hearty and good. He lives and spends a good deal of time with a Hungarian Countess Erdödy who lives in the front part of the large house. But he has

81 Anna Marie Countess Erdödy with her husband Count Peter Erdödy; anonymous painting destroyed in 1945.

become quite estranged from Prince Lichnowsky who lives in the upper part of the same house, although some years ago they were on very intimate terms. I wanted also to call on the Prince, who is an old acquaintance of mine, and on his wife, the daughter of the delightful Countess von Thun, to whom I owe the greatest part of my pleasure during my first visit to Vienna. But I found neither of them at home, and I soon found out that the Princess lives a very retired life.

5 December 1808.

I was invited to another most agreeable dinner by means of a very friendly note from Beethoven, who had not been able to reach me in person. It was given by his hostess, Countess Erdödy. I was so deeply touched there that my pleasure was nearly ruined. Imagine a very pretty, small, delicate woman of twenty-five who had been married at the age of fifteen, had contracted an incurable illness at the time of her first confinement, and in the ten years since then has not been able to remain out of bed for more than two or three months. And yet she has given birth to three healthy and charming children who are as close to her as burs. The only pleasure left for her is music and she plays even Beethoven's music quite well, hobbling from one Forte piano to the other on her still very swollen feet. Withal she is so cheerful, so friendly and kind, that it frequently made me very sad during the otherwise so very pleasant dinner among six or eight good musical souls. And then we got the temperamental Beethoven to the Fortepiano as well. He improvised for a good hour from the depths of his artistic feelings, ranging from the highest heights to the deepest depths of the celestial art, with mastery and versatility, so that ten times at least tears came to my eyes. At the end, I could find no words to express my deep-felt rapture. I hung around his neck like an ardently emotional child, and again was childishly pleased that he and the other enthusiastic souls also seemed to enjoy my Goethe songs.

Reichardt I, 124 f., 147 f.

> Beethoven had meanwhile been composing many masterpieces which needed to be presented to the public, and on 22 December 1808, at the Theater an der Wien, he gave a stupendous evening in which the world heard for the first time the Fifth Symphony, the Sixth Symphony, the Choral Fantasy, the Piano Concerto in G, Op. 58, and several movements of the Mass for Princess Esterházy, Op. 86.

Ferdinand Ries describes Beethoven's concert on 22 December 1808:

Beethoven gave [on 22 December 1808] a large concert in the Theater an der Wien at which were performed for the first time the C Minor and Pastoral Symphonies as well as his Fantasia for Piano with orchestra and chorus. In this last work, at the place where the last beguiling theme appears already in a varied form, the clarinet player made, by mistake, a repeat of eight bars. Since only a few instruments were playing, this error was all the more evident to the ear. Beethoven leaped up in a fury, turned around and abused the orchestra players in the coarsest terms and so loudly that he could be heard throughout the auditorium. Finally, he shouted 'From the beginning!' The theme began again, everyone came in properly, and the success was great. But when the concert was finished the artists, remembering only too well the honourable title which Beethoven had bestowed on them in public, fell into a great rage, as if the offence had just occurred. They swore that they would never play again if Beethoven were in the orchestra, and so forth. This went on until Beethoven had composed something new, and then their curiosity got the better of their anger.

Kerst I, 96.

82 Theater an der Wien; coloured engraving after J. Alt, *c.* 1815.

Johann Friedrich Reichardt describes the concert on 22 December 1808:

Vienna, 25 December 1808.
During this past week, when the theatres were closed and the evenings were taken up with musical performances and concerts, my eagerness and resolution to hear everything caused me no small embarrassment. This was particularly the case on the 22nd, because the local musicians gave the first of the season's great musical performances in the Burg-theater for the benefit of their admirable Society for Musicians' Widows; on the same day, however, Beethoven also gave a concert for his own benefit in the large suburban theatre, consisting entirely of his own compositions. I could not possibly miss this and accepted with heartfelt gratitude Prince Lobkowitz's kind invitation to take me with him in his box. There we held out in the bitterest cold from half-past six until half-past ten, and experienced the fact that one can easily have too much of a good – and even more of a strong – thing. I, no more than

127

the extremely kindly and gentle Prince, whose box was in the first tier very near to the stage, on which the orchestra with Beethoven conducting were quite close to us, would have thought of leaving the box before the very end of the concert, although several faulty performances tried our patience to the utmost. Poor Beethoven, for whom this concert provided the first and only small profit that he had been able to earn and retain during this whole year, had encountered a great deal of opposition and very little support both in its organization and performance. The singers and the orchestra were assembled from very heterogeneous elements. Moreover, it had not even been possible to arrange a complete rehearsal of all the pieces to be performed, every one of which was filled with passages of the utmost difficulty. You will be amazed [to hear] all that was performed by this fertile genius and untiring worker, in the course of four hours.

Reichardt I, 205.   Kerst I, 132 f.

Louis Spohr describes Beethoven conducting:

Seyfried, to whom I expressed my astonishment at this extraordinary method of conducting, told me about a tragi-comical incident which took place during Beethoven's last concert in the Theater an der Wien [1808].

Beethoven was playing a new piano concerto of his, but already at the first *tutti*, forgetting that he was the soloist, he jumped up and began to conduct in his own peculiar fashion. At the first *sforzando* he threw out his arms so wide that he knocked over both the lamps from the music stand of the piano. The audience laughed and Beethoven was so beside himself over this disturbance that he stopped the orchestra and made them start again. Seyfried, worried for fear that this would happen again in the same place, took the precaution of ordering two choirboys to stand next to Beethoven and to hold the lamps in their hands. One of them innocently stepped closer and followed the music from the piano part. But when the fatal *sforzando* burst forth, the poor boy received from Beethoven's right hand such a sharp slap in the face that, terrified, he dropped the lamp on the floor. The other, more wary boy, who had been anxiously following Beethoven's movements, succeeded in avoiding the blow by ducking in time. If the audience had laughed the first time, they now indulged in a truly bacchanalian riot. Beethoven broke out in such a fury that when he struck the first chord of the solo he broke six strings. Every effort of the true music-lovers to restore calm and attention remained unavailing for some time; thus the first Allegro of the Concerto was completely lost to the audience. Since this accident, Beethoven wanted to give no more concerts.

Louis Spohr, *Selbstbiographie, 1860–61*, new edition, Brunswick 1954, p. 200 f. (English transl. London 1865). Kerst I, 174. (The composer Spohr lived in Vienna from 1812 to 1816 and knew Beethoven during those years.)

Anton Schindler discusses the Pastoral Symphony:

The Pastoral, as well as the **C Minor** Symphony, were written in Heiligenstadt, in the place already familiar to the reader from the events of 1802. This village, lying on the right bank of the Danube, was in those years the customary summer resort of our master. Only many years later did he choose places to the south of the capital city, such as Hetzendorf, Mödling or Baden, as his Tusculum, the latter two towns being recommended by his doctors on account of their thermal baths.

In the second half of April 1823, a period of many tribulations and reverses, Beethoven one day proposed a holiday expedition to the north side where he had not set foot for ten years. We decided to go first to Heiligenstadt and its charming surroundings, where he had put so many musical works to paper, and where he had also made many studies of nature. The sun was shining as in summer and the countryside was already clad in its best spring finery. After we had seen the baths of Heiligenstadt with their adjoining gardens and other pleasant sights, and reminisced the while about the works which he had created there, we continued our excursion to the Kahlenberg in the direction of Grinzing. As we walked along the pleasant grassy valley between Heiligenstadt and Grinzing, which is traversed by a softly murmuring brook flowing rapidly down from the nearby hills, shaded in places by tall elm trees, Beethoven frequently stopped and, filled with happy feelings of rapture, let his gaze wander over the beautiful landscape. Then he sat down in a field, leaning against an elm, and asked me if any yellow-hammers were to be heard in the upper branches of these trees. But all was quiet. Thereupon he said, 'This is where I composed the scene by the stream and the yellow-hammers up there, and the quails, the nightingales and the cuckoos round about composed with me.' To my question as to why he had not introduced the yellow-hammers into the scene, he reached for his sketch-book and wrote:

'That is the lady composer up there,' he said, 'and does she not play a more important rôle than the others? For *them*, it is only a game.'. . . .

The Viennese music-lovers of that time had guessed fairly easily, without explanations by the composer, his intentions in this movement [Third Movement, 'Merrymaking of the Country Folk by a Stream']. They apparently recognized, in the form of the first part in three-four time, a version of Austrian country dance music, if not almost a parody of it such as a Beethoven could have written. . . .

The Pastoral Symphony! As the painter completes each element and brings the whole into a united picture, so also did Beethoven in this tone painting. It begins peacefully enough in the foreground; the manifold parts are always resolved quietly. After the terrifying and fearsome depiction of the thunderstorm, the background again resolves itself peacefully, and when in the final measures the distant note of the hunting horn is heard, we feel as if we were in the great concert hall of nature. Praise be to thee, exalted master! Schindler I, 153 ff.

Letter about Beethoven from Stephan von Breuning to Dr Franz Wegeler, from Vienna:

[13 November 1804]
. . . The friend, who remained from the years of my youth here, is still often the cause of my being obliged to neglect the absent ones. You would not believe, my dear Wegeler, what an indescribable and, I might say, ghastly effect the loss of hearing has had on him. Imagine to yourself what the feeling of being a victim of misfortune can do to his vehement character, namely reserve, mistrust, often towards his best friends, and indecision in many things. On the whole, with only a few exceptions when he gives expression to his original spirit, to be with him is truly an effort, wherein one can never trust oneself. From May until the beginning of this month we lived in the same house, and on the very first days I took him into my room. He has hardly been with me when he came down with a very serious passing illness, bordering on the fatal, which finally turned into a continuous intermittent fever. (His chronic tendency to liver malfunction from old times is still noticeable.) Worry and nursing rather took it out of me. Now he is quite well again. He lives on the *Bastei*, while I live in a house recently built by Prince Esterházy in front of the Alser barracks. Since I keep house for myself, he has his meals with me every day.

Breuning 38 f. (The sentence within parenthesis was added by Dr Gerhard von Breuning, Stephan's son.)

83 Jerome Bonaparte; oil portrait by Antoine Jean Gros.

84 Ferdinand Bonaventura Prince Kinsky; anonymous oil portrait.

Never adept at managing his own finances, Beethoven began seriously to worry about his future. He had no steady income, and Mozart's death in dire poverty was obviously a spectre that haunted Vienna for many years after. Now there came a glowing offer from Napoleon's brother, Jerome Bonaparte, King of Westphalia at Cassel. It would have meant a regular yearly income of 600 gold ducats, and Beethoven accepted early in January 1809. His Viennese friends and patrons were aghast, and Countess Erdödy, as well as another intimate friend of Beethoven's, Baron Ignaz von Gleichenstein, worked out a contract for which undoubtedly the Archduke Rudolph was responsible. Under the terms of this contract, dated 1 March 1809, Beethoven was provided with a yearly income of 4000 gulden, guaranteed by the Archduke, Prince Lobkowitz, and another distinguished patron, Ferdinand Bonaventura, Prince Kinsky. As a result of the Napoleonic Wars, and because Prince Lobkowitz and Prince Kinsky soon died (Kinsky in 1812 and Lobkowitz in 1816), Beethoven's financial position was only temporarily improved. But Princess Kinsky proved to be honourable as well as generous, as did the Lobkowitz estate; Beethoven was therefore never really penniless, though he never had much money after the Congress of Vienna in 1815.

Letter from Beethoven to the publishers Breitkopf und Härtel:

Vienna, 7 January 1809

. . . I have at last been obliged by intrigues, cabals and underhanded actions of all kinds to abandon the last remaining German part of my fatherland. His Royal Majesty, the King of Westphalia [Jerome Bonaparte] has offered me the post of Kapellmeister with a yearly stipend of 600 gold ducats. I have today sent by post my assurance that I will accept, and now await the decree of my appointment, following which I will make my travel preparations which should take me through Leipzig – therefore, in order that my journey may be more brilliant for me, please, if this is not otherwise disadvantageous to you, do not make any of my works known until Easter. . . .

With my respects,
your devoted servant,
Beethoven.

[Written on the back of the envelope]:
Please do not make any definite public statement about my appointment in Westphalia until I write to you that I have received the decree. May things go well with you and please write to me soon – we will discuss my compositions in Leipzig – a few hints could be dropped in the Musikalische Zeitung about my departure from here, and perhaps a dig or two, since no one has ever wanted to do anything here to my advantage — —

KAL 245 ff.   Anderson 192.

Letter from Beethoven to Baron Ignaz von Gleichenstein:

[Vienna, February 1809]

It is probably too late to do anything today – I have been unable to get back your written statement from the A[rchduke] until this minute, because his H[ighness] wanted to add a few more items and buts and whereas's. I beg of you to see that the whole refers to the true practice of my art as is proper to me, for then you will have written fully what is in my heart and my head. The introduction states what I receive in Westphalia, 600 ♯ in gold, 150 ♯ travel expenses and for that I must conduct only the concerts for the King, which are short and actually infrequent. I am not even bound to conduct an opera of my composition. From all this it is clear that I can entirely fulfil the most important aspects of my art, to write great works – and also have an orchestra at my disposal. . . .

N.B. We must have the document by 12 noon tomorrow, because we must go to Kinsky's at that time – I hope to see you today.

KAL 241. Anderson 195. (# = ducat.)

Letter from Beethoven to Baron Ignaz von Gleichenstein:

[Vienna, February 1809]

Countess Erdödy thinks that you should draw up a plan with her, whereby, if she is approached, as she believes she undoubtedly will be, she will be in a position to negotiate.

Your friend,
Lu. Beethoven.

If you had time this afternoon, it would give the Countess pleasure to see you.

KAL 255. Anderson 198.

Contract between Beethoven and his patrons:

[stamp of 4 gulden]

Contract.

The daily demonstrations which Herr Ludwig van Beethoven gives of his extraordinary talent and genius as a musical artist and composer have aroused the desire that he may surpass the great expectations warranted by the experiences heretofore achieved.

Since, however, it has been demonstrated that only a man as free from cares as possible can devote himself to one profession excluding all other occupations, and thus be enabled to create great and sublime works ennobling the arts, therefore the undersigned have come to a decision to place Herr Ludwig van Beethoven in the position wherein his most pressing requirements will not be of embarrassment to him, nor in any way inhibit his powerful genius.

They accordingly bind themselves to pay him the yearly fixed sum of 4000 (four thousand) gulden, in the following proportions:

His Imperial Highness, the Archduke Rudolph	Fl.	1500
The Noble Prince Lobkowitz	,,	700
The Noble Prince Ferdinand Kinsky	,,	1800
Total	Fl.	4000

upon which Herr Ludwig van Beethoven can draw half-yearly from each of these noble contracting parties in the amount of his contribution, upon release of a receipt therefor.

133

85 Caroline Marie Princess Kinsky with her sons Rudolph and Joseph; anonymous etching, 1827.

86 Concert at the Malfattis'; anonymous oil painting. In the centre are Therese at the piano and her sister Anna; standing behind Therese, with music in his hands, is Dr Giovanni von Malfatti, who was Beethoven's doctor for a time and attended him on his deathbed.

The undersigned are also willing to continue this annual subsidy until Herr Ludwig van Beethoven obtains an appointment which will pay him a stipend equivalent to the above stated amount.

In the event that such an appointment should not come about, or that Herr Ludwig van Beethoven, through unfortunate circumstances or old age, should be prevented from practising his art, the partners grant him this stipend for the rest of his natural life.

In return, however, Herr Ludwig van Beethoven binds himself to reside in Vienna where the noble contracting parties reside, or to fix on another city situated within the hereditary dominions of His Austrian Imperial Majesty, and to leave such a residence only for stated periods as may be dictated by reason of business or in connection with the encouragement of art, after informing the noble contracting parties of such intended departure, and obtaining the approval thereof.

Thus presented, in Vienna, on 1 March 1809.
[seal] [signed] Rudolph,
                 Archduke.

[seal] [signed]   Prince von Lobkowitz,
                          Duke of Raudnitz.
[seal] [signed]   Ferdinand Prince Kinsky.

[This document bears the following words written in Beethoven's hand:]

Received
on 26 February 1809
from the hands
of the Archduke
Rudolph K. H.

TDR III, 125. (K. H. means Königliche Hoheit.)

Among Beethoven's circle of acquaintances in Vienna was the Malfatti family from Lucca. Dr Giovanni von Malfatti was a famous physician, and Beethoven fell in love with his niece Therese. Her younger sister Anna married Beethoven's intimate friend, Ignaz von Gleichenstein, in 1811. When the Malfattis refused to allow Therese to marry Beethoven, the composer broke off relations, and it was not until Beethoven lay dying that Dr von Malfatti came to see his former patient.

Letter from Beethoven to Therese von Malfatti:

[Vienna, 1 May 1810]

You receive here, honoured Therese, what I promised you, and had there not been certain weighty obstacles, you would have received still more, if only to show you that I always do more for my friends than what I promise them – I hope, and have no doubt, that you are agreeably occupied as well as entertained – the latter not too much, so that we too may be remembered. It would be laying too much stress on you, or setting my worth too high, if I were to apply to you the saying, 'People are united not only when they are together; the distant one and even the departed one is here with us'. Who would wish to apply such a saying to the flighty T[herese] who treats everything in life so lightly?....

Please commend me to the goodwill of your father [and] your mother, although I have as yet no right to claim this and likewise to your cousin M. And now all good wishes to you, honoured T. – I wish you everything good and beautiful in life. Remember me and with fondness – forget the madman – rest assured that no one can desire you to have a merrier and happier life than I do and even when you do not take any interest

in your devoted servant and friend
Beethoven.

TDR III, 209. Anderson 258.

Dr Franz Gerhard Wegeler recalls Beethoven's intention to marry:

It appears, to be sure, that Beethoven once in his life had the intention of marrying, after having often had love affairs, as the saying goes. This intention was evident to many persons, who, like me, read his letter of 10 May [actually 2 May] 1810, wherein Beethoven requested me to obtain for him his baptismal certificate. He said he would repay me for all the expenses, including the cost of travel from Coblenz to Bonn. There follow explicit instructions that in my search for the certificate I should take good care to obtain the right one. I found the solution to this puzzle in a letter from my brother-in-law St. v. Breuning written three months later. In this he said, 'Beethoven tells me at least once a week that he will write to you: personally I think that *his marriage plans have come to nought*, and so he does not feel the urgency of thanking you for obtaining the baptismal certificate.' Beethoven at the age of 39 had consequently not yet abandoned the idea of marriage.

TDR III, 211 f.

87 Pencil drawing of Beethoven by Ludwig Schnorr von Carolsfeld, *c.* 1808 (original disappeared).

Schindler writes about Beethoven's reconciliation with Malfatti:

[In December 1826] Beethoven remembered his former friend, Dr Malfatti, who had become a very celebrated physician, from whom he had been estranged twelve years before and to whom he had not addressed a single word since then. He now placed all his hopes for recovery on this man. But Malfatti would not listen to the master's appeal which I transmitted to him, and coldly turned it down. I made a second and even a third attempt to arouse his compassion for the ailing composer. Finally, I succeeded in persuading him to grant the patient the pleasure of a visit, as if he were making a call to the sick-bed of a stranger. At Malfatti's expressed desire this visit was to take place in the presence of the physician in charge of the case. This, however, was not in accordance with Beethoven's wishes: he wanted to see his former friend alone and to effect a reconciliation. A white lie achieved its aim. Malfatti appeared but did not find his colleague; instead he found the open arms of the remorseful friend who begged forgiveness. All the past was forgotten. From that day onward, Malfatti came almost every day together with Wawruch to [Beethoven's] bedside.   Schindler II, 135.

Dr Bertolini writes about Beethoven's friendship with the Malfattis and with other ladies:

In the company of his intimate friends, Beethoven was extremely cheerful and uninhibited, full of jocose ideas, particularly at a ball given in honour of Malfatti in 1815, for which he had composed a cantata (on a text by Bondi, now in the possession of Miss Belville in London). . . .

Beethoven generally had a 'flame', la Guiccardi [sic], Frau von Frank, Bettina [von] Brentano. But he also often had 'affairs' which did not always turn out very well for him.

Kerst II, 193. (The Cantata was *Un lieto brindisi*, WoO 103.)

> In May 1809, Napoleon again invaded Vienna at the head of the French troops; but this time, Vienna resisted and Napoleon bombarded the city. Haydn died peacefully on 31 May, while Beethoven was composing the 'Emperor' Concerto. Napoleon set up headquarters in Schönbrunn Palace and a concert was given there in his honour, to which Beethoven was not invited.

Ferdinand Ries writes about Beethoven during the bombardment:

[Beethoven fled to the Rauhensteingasse and] spent most of the time in the cellar with his brother Caspar, where he covered his head with pillows in order not to hear the cannon.

WRBN 121. TDR III, 138.

88 Elisabeth (Bettina) von Brentano; drawing by L.E. Grimm, *c.* 1809. She amused Beethoven and helped him to get over his unsuccessful love affair with Therese von Malfatti.

89 Franz Dominik Maria Joseph von Brentano; oil portrait by J.C. Stieler, 1808. He and his young Viennese wife Antonia were close friends of Beethoven's.

90 Antonia Josepha von Brentano, *née* von Birkenstock; anonymous miniature.

While Beethoven was getting over his love affair with Therese von Malfatti, he was consoled by the friendship of the vivacious Bettina von Brentano, with whom Goethe was also on friendly terms.

Letter from Bettina von Brentano to Prince von Pückler-Muskau (1810):

People were astonished to see me arrive hand in hand with Beethoven at a reception of more than forty people who were seated at tables. He took his place without ceremony, spoke but little because he is deaf; twice he took his notebook out of his pocket and wrote down a couple of figures in it. After dinner the whole company climbed up to the top of the tower of the house in order to look at the view. When they had all gone down again and he and I were alone, he took out his notebook, looked over it, wrote and erased things in it and then said to me, 'My song is finished.' He sat down by the window and sang the whole song out into the open air. Then he said, 'It sounds well, doesn't it? It belongs to you, if you like it. I wrote it for you. You incited me to it, I read it in your eyes as if it had all been written down. . . .'

A lady from the upper ranks of society, one of the foremost pianists, performed one of his sonatas. After he had listened to her for a while, he said, 'That's nothing.' He sat down at the piano himself and played the same sonata; it was superhuman.

TDR III, 219 f. (Bettina Brentano, the half-sister of Beethoven's friend Franz Brentano, and wife of Ludwig Joachim von Arnim, maintained a considerable correspondence with Prince Pückler-Muskau, a great admirer of beautiful women. The Prince also boasted of the friendship of Countess Giulietta Guicciardi.)

Herr von Brentano on the friendly relations between Beethoven and his family:

The friendly relations of Beethoven with the Brentano family of Frankfurt/Main concern:

Frau Antonie Brentano, née Birkenstock, born in Vienna 28 May 1780, married there on 23 July 1798, died in Frankfurt/Main on 12 May 1869, and her husband Herr Franz Brentano, merchant, later Juryman and Senator of the Free City of Frankfurt, born in Frankfurt 17 November 1765, died there on 28 June 1844.

These relations had their origin in the friendly intercourse between Beethoven and

Imperial Aulic Councillor Johann Melchior von Birkenstock of Vienna, born in Heiligenstadt im Eichsfeld 11 May 1738, married 1 March 1778 to Carolina Josepha von Hay, widower since 18 March 1788, died in Vienna 30 October 1809;

which had existed since the time when Frau Brentano visited her father in Vienna, whence she had moved with her older children in 1809 for a long period because her father, Aulic Councillor von Birkenstock, had been seriously ill for some time. This relationship continued also after the death on 30 October 1809 of Aulic Councillor von Birkenstock, during the three years that the Brentano family lived in Vienna. Beethoven was a frequent guest in the Birkenstock, later Brentano, house, where he attended the quartet-playing of the excellent Viennese musicians and where he often gave pleasure to his friends with his wonderful playing. The Brentano children sometimes brought fruit and flowers to his apartment; in return he would regale them with sweets, and he treated them with the greatest friendliness.

TDR III, 216. (This ancient Italian family hardly made use of their title.)

Carl Czerny writes about Beethoven and the Brentano children:

Today Court Councillor Witteschek/: who knew Beethoven well:/ told me that in the year 1814, B:/who could then still hear fairly well:/ very often went to the Brentano-Birkenstock house, and that once one of the members of the family, an eight-year-old girl, whom he had been teasing, in a fit of childish caprice suddenly emptied a bottle of ice-cold water over his head, when he was overheated. From then on, there developed the diseased condition which led to his complete deafness.

Note by Schindler: This occurrence dates back to the year 1812, when Frau von Brentano-B[irkenstock] visited Vienna for the last time with her little daughter (now Frau von Blattersdorf, [wife of] the former Minister of Baden), as she herself told me. To ascribe such consequences to a dousing with cold water is not acceptable, since B[eethoven] was able to hear music quite well for some years after that, and also in 1814 himself played his new Trio Opus 97 in public twice. This little Brentano-B[irkenstock] is the 'little friend' to whom B. dedicated one or two of the little Rondos.

A. Schindler.

Czerny 18.

In the summer of 1811, Beethoven went to Teplitz, where he met a group of interesting people, among them Karl August Varnhagen von Ense, Rahel Levin, and Amalie Sebald. In Teplitz again the next year, he finally met Goethe. Goethe was rather wary of Beethoven but found his piano-playing 'delightful'. In July 1812 Beethoven wrote his famous letters to the 'immortal beloved' and then went on to Karlsbad and from there to Linz, where he visited his brother Johann, who had an apothecary shop .in that pretty Upper-Austrian town on the Danube. At Linz, Beethoven completed his Eighth Symphony. The work was not, however, performed until 27 February 1814.

Letter from Karl August Varnhagen von Ense to Ludwig Uhland about Beethoven at Teplitz:

[1811]

In the last days of the waning summer at Teplitz, I made the acquaintance of Beethoven and found this reputedly savage and unsociable man to be the most magnificent artist with a heart of gold, a glorious spirit and a friendly disposition. What he has refused to princes he granted to us at first sight: he played on the Fortepiano. I soon was on intimate terms with him and his noble character, the uninterrupted flow of a godlike spirit which I always seemed to feel with an almost reverential awe when in his very silent presence, drew me closely to him, to such an extent that day after day, especially the last one [before his departure], I did not ever feel the burden of his company which, on account of his deafness, tended to be rather exhausting. I spent the time entirely with him and his friend Oliva. The latter is one of the best of men, whom Kerner also knew. If I had not already known, from unimpeachable sources, that Beethoven is the greatest, most profound and prolific of German composers, the mere sight of his appearance would have convinced me, who am otherwise ignorant of music, beyond any doubt: He lives only for his art and no earthly passion can still the music within him. He is incredibly industrious and prolific. On his walks he seeks out distant places along lonely paths between the mountains and through the forests, finding peace in the contemplation of the great features of nature, and thinking in musical tones: this brings happiness into his heart. I mention these things so that you will not attempt to compare him to any other musician but will place him in a category by himself. If I could only tell you how beautiful, how moving, devout and serious, as if he had been kissed by a God, this man appeared as he played for us on the Fortepiano some heavenly variations, pure creations granted by God to which the artist must give voice and, much as he would have wished, could not fix down on paper! At his request, my dear friend, I gave him all your poems, which there was no time to copy. So you can hope soon to see some of them set to music. I am as happy about this as if they were my own.

Kerst I, 168 f. *Echo*, No. 4, 1886.

91 View of Bad Teplitz, where Beethoven took a six weeks' cure in 1811; anonymous watercolour.

Karl August Varnhagen von Ense recalls a meeting with Beethoven (1811):

But at the same time I made the acquaintance of a musician who put the other [Himmel] quite in the shade. This was Beethoven, of whose presence [in Teplitz] we had known for a long time, although no one had as yet seen him. His deafness made him unsociable and his peculiarities which, due to his isolation, grew ever sharper, made the limited intercourse with whomever he happened to meet by accident difficult and short. He had, however, seen Rahel* a few times during his lonely walks in the castle gardens and he had noticed her facial expression, which in certain aspects recalls his own. An amiable young man called Oliva, who accompanied him as a faithful friend, easily arranged an introduction. What Beethoven obstinately refused, even when insistently requested; what on one fearful occasion a Prince tried to oblige him to do, attempting by physical force to make him play to his guests; what no violence could bully him into doing, he now granted gladly and

* Rahel Levin, who was later (27 September 1814) married to Varnhagen. (Otto Verdrow, *Rahel Varnhagen*, Berlin 1900, p. 113)

generously. He sat down at the Fortepiano and played his still unknown newest compositions, or else engaged in free improvisation. To me, the man meant even more than the artist, and since an intimate friendship sprang up between Oliva and myself, I was with Beethoven almost daily. I was able to engage in closer relations with him through his eagerly expressed hope that I might procure or adapt texts for dramatic compositions. That Beethoven has a violent hatred for the French and is very German in his feelings is well known, and this also brought us close to one another.

Kerst I, 167. K. A. Varnhagen von Ense: *Denkwürdigkeiten*, II, 344.

Letter from Johann Wolfgang von Goethe to his friend Carl Friedrich Zelter:

[2 September 1812]

I met Beethoven in Töplitz [Teplitz]. His talent astounded me; but unfortunately he is a quite intractable person, which in fact is not unjustified if he finds the world detestable; but as a result, of course, he does not make things more enjoyable either for himself or for others. He is much to be forgiven and also to be pitied, since he can hear nothing. This is perhaps less harmful to the musical than to the social part of his life. And being by nature laconic, he feels this defect twice as much.

Kerst I, 169. (Zelter was the director of the Berlin *Singakademie*.)

From Johann Wolfgang von Goethe's diary:

20 July [1812] . . . in the evening went with Beethoven to Bilin.

21 July . . . evening at Beethoven's. He played delightfully.

Letter about Beethoven from Goethe to his wife, 19 July 1812:

I have never before seen a more comprehensive, energetic or intense artist. I understand very well how strange he must appear to the outside world.

Kerst I, 169.

Anton Schindler on Beethoven's appearance:

Beethoven could not have been much more than 5 feet 4 inches tall, Viennese measure. His body was thick-set, with large bones and a strong muscular system; his head was unusually large, covered with long, unkempt, almost completely grey hair, giving him a somewhat savage aspect, enhanced even more when his beard had grown to an immoderate length, which was quite often the case. His forehead was high and broad, his brown eyes small, almost retreating into his head when he laughed.

92 Ludwig van Beethoven; bronze bust by Franz Klein, based on a life-mask Klein made in 1812. It is therefore probably the most accurate representation of Beethoven's features.

They could, however, suddenly become unusually prominent and large, either rolling and flashing – the pupils almost always turned upwards – or not moving at all, staring fixedly ahead when one or another idea took hold of him. When that happened, his whole appearance would suddenly and conspicuously alter, with such a noticeably inspired and imposing look that his small figure would loom before one as gigantically as his spirit. These moments of sudden inspiration often befell him in even the most jovial company, but also in the street, which generally attracted the close attention of passers-by. Only his gleaming eyes and his face showed what was going on inside him; he never gesticulated with his head or his hands, except when leading an orchestra. His mouth was well formed, the lips even (it is said that when he was young the lower lip was somewhat prominent), the nose rather broad. With his smile a most benevolent and amiable air spread over his whole face; this was of special benefit when he conversed with strangers, for it encouraged them. His laughter, on the other hand, often burst out immoderately, distorting the intelligent and strongly marked features; the huge head would swell, the face would become still broader, and the

whole effect was not seldom that of a grimacing caricature. Fortunately, it always passed quickly. The chin had a longish cleft in the middle and at both sides, which gave it the shape of a mussel-shell and a special peculiarity of its own. His complexion was yellowish, but this was less obvious due to his being so much out of doors, particularly during the summer; then his full cheeks took on a fresh red and brown coloration.
Schindler, *Beethoven*, 2nd ed., 1845, p. 269. Kerst II, 19 f.

Letters to the 'immortal beloved' :

Morning of 6 July [1812]

My angel, my all, my other self, just a few words today and that in pencil (yours); only tomorrow will I know for certain where I am to stay, a worthless waste of time and such – why this deep sorrow when necessity speaks? Can our love exist other than by sacrifices, by not desiring everything? Can you help it that you are not all mine, that I am not all yours? Oh God, look at the loveliness of nature and calm your spirit about what has to be – love demands everything, and perfectly rightly, that is how it is with me about you, with you about me – except that you forget so easily that I must live for me and for you. If we could be united, you would feel this pain as little as I. The journey was terrible – I did not arrive here until 4 in the morning. There were not enough horses, so the post coach took another route, but what a terrible one. At the second-last station they warned me against travelling at night and tried to frighten me about a forest, but that only tempted me – – – and I was in the wrong. The coach had to go and break down on such a terrible road, for no reason, just a country road. Without the postillions I had, I would have been held up completely on the way. The same thing happened to Esterházi, who took the normal route with 8 horses, as happened to me with four – however, it was partly enjoyable for me, as it is every time I survive something that turns out well. And now quickly from externals to more intimate things. We will surely see one another soon; today, too, I cannot tell you the observations I have been making during the past few days about my life – – – if our hearts were always close to one another I would probably not make any. My heart is full of things to tell you – oh – there are moments when I feel that speech is nothing whatever. Be cheerful, remain my faithful, one and only treasure, my everything, as I am yours; for the rest, the Gods must send what shall be for us. –

Your faithful
Ludwig.

93 View of Karlsbad; coloured engraving by F. W. Rothe from a drawing by J. G. Jentsch. During a second visit to Teplitz in July 1812, Beethoven wrote the first of the three famous letters to the 'Immortal Beloved' who was at that time in Karlsbad.

Monday evening, 6 July

You are suffering, my dearest – I have only just heard that letters must be posted early in the morning. Mondays and Thursdays are the only days the post goes from here to K[arlsbad] – You are suffering – oh, where I am you are with me too, and I will make it possible, for you and me, that I can live with you, and what a life it will be!!! Without you, pursued by the kindness of people here and there, which I think I deserve as little as I want to deserve it. The humility of man towards his fellow-men, it pains me – and when I consider myself as part of the universe, what I am and what He is who is called Greatest – and yet – in it is the divinity of man. I weep when I think that you will probably not receive my first news until Saturday. However much you love me, I love you more – but never hide yourself from me. Good night. Since I am taking the waters I must go to sleep [two words crossed out]. Oh God, so near, so far; is not our love a truly celestial thing – and as strong as the firmament. –

good morning on July 7 –

while still abed my thoughts turn to you, my immortal beloved, some of them happy, some sad, waiting to see whether fate will hear us. I can live only completely with you or not at all; I have decided to stray about in the distance until I can fly to your arms and can regard you as my homeland, and can send my soul, enveloped by you, into the realm of spirits. Yes, it must be – you can compose yourself, all the more since you know my faithfulness towards you; never can another possess my heart, never, never – oh God, why must one leave what one loves so, and yet my life in V[ienna] is wretched as it is now. Your love makes me at once the happiest and unhappiest of men – at my age I need a certain uniform steadiness to my life – can this exist in our relationship? Angel, I have just heard that the post leaves daily, and I must therefore close so that you get the letter as soon as possible. Be calm; only by seeing our situation calmly can we attain our goal of living together. Be calm, love; today, yesterday – what longing with tears for you – you – you – my life, my everything – farewell, oh, go on loving me – never deny the true heart of

yours eternally

mine eternally   Your loving

ours eternally   L.

KAL 71 ff. Anderson 373.

There now began the one period in Beethoven's life when he not only achieved sensational public success with concerts of his new works but also made a very considerable amount of money, which he turned into bank shares and kept all the rest of his life so as to be able to leave it to his nephew Carl. The first of these big concerts took place in the old University in Vienna on 8 December 1813, when the Seventh Symphony and *Wellington's Victory or the Battle at Vittoria* were first performed. This was a charity concert and was repeated on 12 December. In the concerts of 1814 *Wellington's Victory* became the public rage. But Beethoven also had an enormous success with the Seventh Symphony, and later with the Eighth. In May 1814, *Fidelio* was again revised and became as successful as it had been previously unpopular.

Franz Wild about Beethoven's Battle of Vittoria:

One scene has impressed itself imperishably upon my memory. . . . He expressed the wish to conduct his work *The Battle of Vittoria* himself at the first performance. . . . He was allowed to have his wish. He stepped to the podium, and the orchestra, aware of his failings, fell into a state of anxious excitement, which all too soon proved to be justified. Hardly had the music begun, when the creator himself provided a spectacle

94 The old University in Vienna; coloured engraving by Carl Schütz, 1790.

which staggered the senses. In the *piano* parts he sank to his knees, at the *forte* he reached upwards so that, like a dwarf, he would vanish altogether under the conductor's stand, then, like a giant, he would tower above it. All the while his arms and hands would be in motion as if with the music a thousand lives had taken possession of his every limb. At the beginning this did not endanger the effect of the work, for at first the crouching and stretching of his body corresponded respectively to the decrease and the increase of the sound. But suddenly the genius found himself ahead of the orchestra. He became invisible at the *forte* passages and reappeared at the *piano* passages. Danger now threatened, and at the decisive moment Kapellmeister Umlauf took command, making it clear to the orchestra that they should follow him. For a long time Beethoven did not notice anything. When at last he became aware of it, there came to his lips a smile which, if ever it had been my good fortune to see one, deserves the appellation 'heavenly'.

Kerst I, 184 f. (The famous tenor Wild recalled this performance in his autobiography published in *Rezensionen über Theater und Musik*, Vienna 1860, No. 4.)

Report to the Viennese Secret Police:

The English are so religious that they do not listen to music on Sundays.

Therefore the musical Academy of H. v. Beethoven was postponed from Sunday to a weekday. . . . Yesterday's musical Academy did not in any way increase esteem for the talent of H. Beethoven. There are factions pro and contra Beethoven. In contrast to Razumovsky, Apponyi, Kraft, who deify Beethoven, there exists a substantial majority of knowledgeable people who want to hear no music whatsoever by Herr Beethoven.

August Fournier, *Die Geheimpolizei auf dem Wiener Kongress*, Vienna 1913, p. 288. (The Academy, in which Beethoven himself conducted *Der glorreiche Augenblick* [*The Glorious Moment*] and *Die Schlacht bei Vittoria* [*The Battle at Vittoria*], had indeed been postponed from Sunday 27 November to Tuesday 29 November 1814.)

From the diary of Carl Bertuch [*1814*]:

Tuesday, 29 November. Beethoven's twice postponed concert was given at twelve o'clock noon. – 1. A new symphony, distinguished by both its richness and its clarity, and representing a new marvellous enrichment of orchestral music. 2. Cantata, the text of which is extremely mediocre [*Der glorreiche Augenblick*]: all that it really contains is the fact that there are now many sovereigns in Vienna; [it reads] exactly like so many poems written for the occasion. The music is excellent. The song of Vusina with contrasting choruses and Mayseder's playing of the accompaniments were excellent. Bondra and Milder, Forti and Wild sang. *The Battle of Vittoria* [is a] daring musical character picture which begins with the approach of the side drum, then the fanfares sound Rule Britannia, the battle itself with battle fire; finally the roar ceases, except for a few isolated cannon shots – God Save the King. The second part of the *Victory Symphony* was given under Beethoven's direction. *Beethoven's conducting is unique. The outer world is too puny for him; he seeks new realms for his work. Small and large; he crouches and rises physically.* Royalty present: the Emperor Alexander, the Empress of Russia, both Grand-Duchesses, the King of Prussia (who stayed only for the first part), the Royal Prince of Sicily. The hall was very full. . . .

Carl Bertuchs Tagebuch vom Wiener Kongress, edited by Hermann Freiherr von Egloff-stein, Berlin 1916, pp. 59f. (Bertuch was a publisher from Weimar, who tried [1815 in Vienna] to promote a law against piracy.)

Louis Spohr writes about Beethoven's Fidelio:

Beethoven's *Fidelio*, which in the year 1805 had enjoyed very little success because of the unfortunate circumstance of the occupation of Vienna by the French, was now resurrected by the directors of the Kärntnerthortheater and staged for their benefit. Beethoven had been persuaded to add a new overture (in E), an aria for the jailer, and the great aria for Fidelio with the *obbligato* horns, and to make a few changes as well.

In this new version the opera had a great success and enjoyed a long run of very well attended performances. On the first evening the composer was called before the curtain a number of times and was once again the object of general attention.   Louis Spohr, *op. cit.*, p. 199. Kerst I, 173.

Anton Schindler about Prince Lichnowsky:

. . . Prince Lichnowsky was in the habit of visiting his protégé quite often in his study. They mutually agreed that neither was to take any notice of the other's presence, so that the master would not be disturbed. The Prince, after saying 'Good Morning', would leaf through a manuscript, observe the master at work for a while, and would then depart with a friendly 'Adieu'. Even so, Beethoven felt himself disturbed by such a visit, and from time to time he would lock the door. Not taking this amiss, the Prince would descend the flights of stairs. When the servant, who also worked as a tailor, was sitting in the anteroom, his Serene Highness would keep him company and tarry until the door opened and he could give the Prince of the musical art a friendly greeting.   Schindler I, 188.

> Because of his deafness, Beethoven was now just able to play his own chamber music in public: the well-known pianist Ignaz Moscheles was present when Beethoven gave his new 'Archduke' Trio, Op. 97, and made some interesting notes about Beethoven in this period.

Ignaz Moscheles about Beethoven in 1814:

11 April, 1814. At a musical entertainment at the *Römischer Kaiser* given at noon, I heard a new Trio★ by Beethoven in B-Flat Major played by himself. How many compositions are unjustifiably marked with the little word 'new'. But never a composition by Beethoven, and surely not this one, which is completely original. Apart from the spirit, his actual playing gave me less satisfaction, because it was neither clean nor precise, yet I could still notice many traces of a once great virtuosity, which I had long recognized in his compositions.

[1814.] I went early to see Beethoven. He was still in bed. On this day he was in an exceptionally good humour, jumped out of bed and, quite as he was, went and stood by the window, which overlooked the Schottenbastei, to look through the arrangements of the pieces. Quite naturally all the dear street urchins gathered under the window, until

★ The 'Archduke' Trio, Op. 97, dedicated to Archduke Rudolph.

he exclaimed: 'Those damned boys, what do they want?' I pointed smilingly at him. 'Yes, yes, you are right,' he said, and quickly put on a dressing gown.

When we came to the last great duet 'Namenlose Freude', I wrote the text: 'Ret=terin des Gat=ten'; he crossed it out and wrote: 'Rett=erin des Gatt=en'; for it is impossible to sing the consonant 't'. Underneath the last piece I had written: '*fine* with God's help'. He was not at home when I brought it to him. When he sent it back to me, he had written underneath: 'O Man, help thyself.'

Kerst I, 162 f.

Blasius Höfel relates his memories of Beethoven to Alexander Wheelock Thayer:

Höfel saw Beethoven frequently at Artaria's, and when his work was fairly well advanced, he asked him to sit for him once or twice. The request was willingly granted, and at the appointed time the engraver appeared with his plate. Beethoven placed himself in the desired position, and sat still for perhaps five minutes, then he suddenly jumped up, ran to the piano and began to improvise, much to Höfel's discomfiture. The servant tried to help him out, assuring Höfel that he could now sit near the instrument and work at leisure, for the master had completely forgotten him and did not even realize any more that anyone was in the room. This Höfel did. He remained at work as long as he needed, and then left without Beethoven's taking the least notice. The result was satisfactory, since only two sittings of less than one hour each were required.

Kerst I, 180. TDR III, 437 f.

> During the last fifteen years of his life, one of Beethoven's principal Viennese publishers was the firm of Steiner & Co. Between the composer and the publishers there existed a cordial relationship, and the men gave themselves military titles. Beethoven was the 'Generalissimus', Steiner was the 'Lieutenant-General', etc.

Anselm Hüttenbrenner speaking to Alexander Wheelock Thayer:

Beethoven came every week a couple of times to the publishing house Steiner & Co., in the mornings between eleven and twelve o'clock. There a group of composers gathered almost every morning and exchanged musical opinions. Schubert accompanied me several times. We enjoyed Beethoven's pithy and often sarcastic observations, especially when they were about Italian music.

TDR III, 582. Kerst I, 207. (Hüttenbrenner, a friend of Schubert's, was a musician.)

95 Beethoven; engraving by Blasius Höfel from Louis Letronne's pencil drawing (ill. 7), 1814. According to contemporary opinion, this was one of the best portraits of the composer ever made.

From the diary of Dr Carl von Bursy:

Vienna, 1 June [1816]

Beethoven came out of the room next door to meet me. It was difficult and unnatural for me to pay the master of my art only a polite and impersonal compliment. I should have liked to seize his hand and press on it a kiss of the deepest veneration. . . .

Small, rather stocky, hair combed back with much grey in it, a rather red face, fiery eyes which, though small, are deep-set and unbelievably full of life. Beethoven, especially when he laughs, has a great resemblance to Amenda. He asked after him [Amenda] and showed feelings of true friendship for him. 'He is a truly good man,' said he. 'It is my misfortune that all my friends are far away and here I am alone in this hateful Vienna.' He asked me to speak loudly to him because at the moment he again has great difficulties with his hearing, and for that reason wants to go to Baden this summer and be in the country. In general he has not been in good health for some time and has not composed anything new. . . . [They discussed a libretto which Amenda had sent to Beethoven.]

I shouted into his ear that for such tasks one must certainly have plenty of time and inspiration. 'No,' said he, 'I never do anything straight through without pause. I always work on several things at once, and sometimes I work on this one and sometimes on that one.' He misunderstood me very often and had to use the utmost concentration, when I was speaking, to get my meaning. That, of course, embarrassed and disturbed me very much. It disturbed him, too, and this led him to speak more himself and very loudly. He told me a lot about his life and about Vienna. He was venomous and embittered. He raged about everything, and is dissatisfied with everything, and he curses Austria and Vienna in particular. He speaks quickly and with great vivacity. He often banged his fist on the piano and made such a noise that it echoed around the room. He is not exactly reserved; for he told me about his personal affairs and related much about himself and his family. That is precisely the *signum diagnosticum* of hypochondria. I was rather pleased with this hypochondria, because I learned so much about his life from his very lips. He complains about the present age, and for many reasons. Art no longer occupies a position high above the commonplace, art is no longer held in such high esteem and particularly not as regards recompense. Beethoven complains of bad times in a pecuniary sense. Can one believe that a Beethoven has grounds for such complaints?

'Why do you stay in Vienna when every foreign potentate would be glad to give you a place at his court or next to his throne?' 'Certain conditions keep me here', said he, 'but everything here is mean and dirty. Things could not be worse. From top to bottom everything is shabby. You can't trust anyone. What is not written down in black and white, no one will honour. They want your work and then pay you a beggar's pittance, not even what they agreed to pay. . . .'

His lodgings are pleasant and look out over the green *Bastei*. The rooms are well appointed and decently furnished. A bedroom opens out of the entrance hall, on the other side is a music room with a closed piano in it. I saw very little music, there were a few sheets of music paper on the desk. Two good oil portraits were on the wall, a man and a woman.

Petersburger Zeitung, 1854, Nos. 78 and 79.   Kerst I, 198 ff. (Dr Carl von Bursy was a friend of Amenda's and came with his recommendation to see Beethoven in 1816.)

Louis Schlösser describes Beethoven's appearance in about 1822:

A few weeks later we met on the Kärnthnerstrasse; with his sharp eye he had seen me first. He came up to me and took my arm with the following words: 'If you have time, come with me to the Paternoster-gässel to Steiner's (the music shop of Steiner & Haslinger), and I will read him the riot act; these publishers always have every kind of sub-terfuge up their sleeves. When it comes to publishing my compositions, they would just as soon avoid doing this until after my death because they could make more money out of them; but I shall know how to deal with them.' (This is word for word.) At this meeting I was quite

96 Beethoven; plaster bust by Anton Dietrich (detail). An inscription on the pedestal informs us that it was modelled from life in 1821.

astonished to notice that Beethoven, usually so careless about his dress, appeared in a most unusually elegant attire: blue tail-coat with yellow buttons, immaculate white trousers, a matching waistcoat, and a new beaver hat worn as usual towards the back of his head. I left him at the entrance of the shop, which was crowded with people, and he thanked me for my company and went with Herr Steiner to his office. I could not avoid reporting to my teacher Mayseder, who lived nearby, the remarkable metamorphosis of Beethoven's elegance, an occurrence which surprised him less than myself, for he told me with a smile, 'That's not the first time his friends have stolen his old clothes during the night and replaced them with new ones; he won't have even noticed it and will have quite happily put on the new clothes which were lying handy.' This is the only remarkable anecdote that I have to tell about him. Nor did I pursue the matter further to find out if this was the way it really happened, but I must repeat that I never noticed Beethoven to be unobservant.

Hallelujah, 4th year, 1885, No. 20/21.   Kerst II, 14 f.

Carl Czerny describes Beethoven's improvisation:

Beethoven's improvisation aroused considerable attention in the first years after his arrival in Vienna, even including the admiration of Mozart. It assumed various forms, depending on whether he improvised on themes of his own or on themes given to him [by others].

First: In the form of a first movement of a sonata or of a rondo finale: the first part would come to a regular close and he would use a related key for the middle melody. In the second part he would give free rein to his improvisation, making, however, every possible use of the main theme. He further enlivened the tempo allegro with *bravura* passages which were generally even more difficult than those found in his [written] compositions.

Second: A free variation form, more or less on the lines of his Choral Fantasia, Op. 89, or the choral finale of the Ninth Symphony, both of which provide an excellent example of the style of his improvisations.

Third: A mixed genre in which one idea would follow another, in the manner of a *pot-pourri*, as in his Fantasia, Op. 77.

A few insignificant notes often sufficed as material for the construction of a whole improvised work, similar to the finale of the Sonata in D Major, Op. 10 No. 3.

When he had finished such improvisations, Beethoven would break out into hearty and satisfied laughter. No one could equal him in the dexterity of his playing of scales, his double trills or his leaps: not even Hummel. His deportment while playing was exemplary: quiet, noble and beautiful. Nor did he indulge in any form of grimace. As his deafness increased, he tended to stoop. His fingers were very strong, not long, and the finger-tips were broadly shaped from much playing. He often told me that in his youth he practised an enormous amount, sometimes until long after midnight. When he taught he also insisted on a proper position of the fingers, according to the school of Emanuel Bach, which he used in teaching me. His own span was barely a tenth. He made considerable use of the pedal, far more than is indicated in his [published] works. His interpretations of the scores of Handel and Gluck and of the Fugues of Johann Sebastian Bach were unique: in the first he knew how to endow them with a full-voiced amplitude and a spirit which gave a new form to these works. He was the greatest sight-reader of his day, even of orchestral scores. As if by divination he could grasp an unfamiliar composition simply by leafing through it at speed. His judgments were always correct yet, especially in his younger years, sharp, biting and inconsiderate. Many works which the world admired, and still admires, he viewed from the high point of view of his genius in quite a different light.

Extraordinary as his improvisation was, his interpretation of those of his own compositions which had already appeared in print was less successful. He would not take enough trouble or time to practise again [something already familiar to him]. The success therefore depended on chance, or on his mood. Since both his playing and his compositions were in advance of his time, so also were the pianofortes of the time (up to 1810) often unequal to carrying his gigantic interpretations, being, as they were, still weak and imperfect. Because of this it came about that Hummel's pearly playing, with its brilliance calculated to a nicety, was far more comprehensible and attractive to the general public.

Nevertheless, Beethoven's interpretation of adagios and his lyric legato style exercised an almost magic spell on everyone who heard him and, to the best of my knowledge, has never been surpassed by anyone.
Czerny 21, 22.

A page from Beethoven's notebook:

My decree is to remain in the country; how easy it is to do that in whatever corner. My unfortunate hearing does not plague me there./ It is as if/ every tree spoke to me/ in the country, holy! holy!/ Ecstasy in the woods! Who/ can describe it?/ If all comes to nought/ the country itself remains/, Gaden, Untere Brühl etc./ in the winter/ it would be easy/ to rent a lodging from a peasant;/ around this time it is/ surely not expensive./ Sweet stillness of the woods! The wind which blows already on the second nice day cannot retain me in Vienna, because it is my enemy.

Theodor Frimmel, *Beethoven Handbuch*, Hildesheim-Wiesbaden 1968, I, 423. (Facsimile in *Ein Wiener Beethovenbuch*, compiled by Alfred Orel, Vienna 1921, p. 231. This autograph was formerly in the possession of Guido Adler, Vienna.)

On 29 November 1814, Beethoven gave a brilliant concert in the Redoutensaal in which the Seventh Symphony was performed and was such a success that the slow movement had to be repeated.

Louis Spohr recalls the concert on 29 November 1814:

His friends grasped this favourable occasion [the success of the revival of *Fidelio*] to organize a concert in the Grand *Redoutensaal*, in which the newest compositions by Beethoven were to be performed. Anybody who could play a string or wind instrument, or sing, was invited to take part, and not one of the leading artists of Vienna was missing. I and my orchestra naturally consented to take part, and for the first time I saw Beethoven conduct. Although much had been told to me about his way of conducting, it nevertheless astounded me in the utmost degree. Beethoven was in the habit of giving dynamic indications to the orchestra by means of all sorts of peculiar movements of his body. When he wanted a *sforzando* he would vehemently throw out both his arms, which previously he had held crossed across his breast. For a *piano* he would crouch down, going down deeper as he wanted the sound to be softer. Then, at the beginning of a *crescendo* he would rise gradually and when the *forte* was reached he would leap up into the air. Occasionally he would shout with the music in order to make the *forte* stronger, without being conscious of it. . . .

The concert organized by his friends enjoyed a most brilliant success. The new compositions by Beethoven were exceptionally well received, particularly the Symphony in A Major (the Seventh); the wonderful second movement had to be repeated; it made a deep and lasting impression on me.

The execution was quite masterly despite Beethoven's uncertain and sometimes ludicrous conducting. It was evident that the poor deaf master was no longer able to hear the *pianos* in his music. This was particularly evident in a passage in the second part of the first *Allegro* of the symphony, where two *fermate* follow one another, of which the second is *pianissimo*. Beethoven probably had overlooked the second one, because he started off beating time again before the orchestra had even begun the second *fermata*. Therefore, without knowing it, he was ahead of the orchestra by as much as ten or twelve bars when it began to play the *pianissimo*. Beethoven, indicating the passage in his own way, had crouched down under the music stand; at the *crescendo*, which followed, he became visible once more, made himself taller, and then leapt high up in the air at the moment when, according to his calculation, the *forte* should have begun. When this did not happen, he looked about him in terror, stared in astonishment at the orchestra, which was still playing the *pianissimo*, and found his place only when the so-long-awaited *forte* began and became audible to him.

Fortunately this comic scene during the performance was not noticed by the audience; otherwise they would have laughed.

Since the hall was completely filled and the applause enthusiastic, Beethoven's friends organized a repetition of the concert, which brought in almost equal profits. By this means Beethoven was spared financial

97 Beethoven; pencil drawing by Carl Friedrich August von Kloeber. This drawing, probably made at Mödling about 1818, appears to have been a study for the large, now lost, painting of Beethoven and his nephew Carl.

embarrassments for a while; yet these recurred once or twice before his death, due to the same reasons. . . .
Louis Spohr, *op. cit.*, pp. 200, 201 f.   Kerst I, 173 ff.

August von Kloeber discusses Beethoven:

A brother-in-law of mine, Baron von Skrbensky, who owned an estate in Austrian Silesia and died many years ago, asked me to do a portrait of Beethoven for him as part of a collection of famous Viennese artists and composers of the time.

Making Beethoven's acquaintance was a difficult task, and it was still more difficult to get him to sit for me. By a fortunate chance I had come to know a friend of Beethoven's, the cellist Dont, a member of the Imperial Court Opera Theatre; this proved to be helpful, the more so as Dont himself was most interested in the plan. Dont advised me to wait until the summer, since Beethoven usually spent the summer in Mödling and was then at his most easy-going and accessible. In a letter, our mutual friend told Beethoven that I would be arriving in Mödling, and also that I wished to draw him. Beethoven agreed, on condition that he would not have to sit for too long at a time.

Early in the morning I went to call on him. His old housekeeper told me he was still at breakfast but would soon be coming; in the meantime there were books by Goethe and Herder with which I could occupy myself. Beethoven finally came in and said, 'You want to paint me, but I am very impatient.' He was already quite deaf, and if I wanted to say something I had to write it, or else he used his ear-trumpet when his *famulus* (a young relation of about twelve [nephew Carl]) was not present to shout the words into his ear.

Beethoven then sat down, and the boy had to begin practising the [Broadwood] piano, a gift from England and equipped with a large metal dome. The instrument stood roughly four to five paces behind him, and Beethoven, despite his deafness, corrected every mistake the boy made, had him repeat single passages, etc.

Beethoven always looked very serious, his extremely lively eyes usually wandered, looking upwards somewhat darkly and low-spiritedly, which I have attempted to capture in the portrait. His lips were shut, but the expression about the mouth was not unfriendly. – One of his favourite topics was the overweening vanity and perverted taste of the Viennese aristocracy, about whom he never had a good word to say, for he considered himself neglected by them, or not sufficiently understood.

After roughly 3/4 of an hour he became restless; remembering Dont's advice, I now knew it was time to stop, and asked him only if I could come again the next day, since I was staying in Mödling. Beethoven was quite agreeable and said, 'Then we can meet more often, for I cannot sit still too long at one time; you must also have a good look at Mödling, for it is quite lovely here, and as an artist you must certainly be a nature-lover.' I encountered Beethoven several times on my walks in Mödling, and it was most interesting to see him, a sheet of music paper and a stump of a pencil in his hand, stop often as though listening, look up and down and then write a few notes on the paper. Dont had told me that when I saw him thus, I should never speak to him or take any notice of him, because that would make him embarrassed or even unpleasant. Once, when setting out on a walk through the woods, I saw him climbing up the hill opposite, from the defile which separated us, his broad-brimmed, grey felt hat pressed under his arm; once at the top, he lay down full length under a pine-tree and looked at the sky for a long while. Every morning he sat a little less than an hour for me. When Beethoven saw my portrait, he mentioned that he liked the way the hair was done; other painters had always done it too elegantly dressed, as though he were appearing before a court official, and he was not like that at all. – I must mention that the oil painting done for my brother-in-law is larger than the lithograph, and that Beethoven is holding a sheet of music in his hand; the background is a Mödling landscape.

Beethoven's dwelling in Mödling was quite simple, as indeed was everything about him; his clothing consisted of a light blue frock-coat with yellow buttons, white waistcoat and necktie, as was then the fashion, but all in a quite neglected state. His complexion was healthy and robust, the skin somewhat pockmarked; his hair was the colour of blued steel, having already begun to change from black to grey. His eyes were blue-grey and quite lively. When his hair was tossed about by the wind, he had something absolutely Ossian-like and demoniacal about him. In friendly conversation, however, he took on a genial and mild expression, particularly when he was pleasantly affected by the subject. Every mood of his spirit was immediately and violently expressed in his countenance.

Allgemeine Musikalische Zeitung, No. 18, 4 May 1864.

One of the Viennese suburbs which Beethoven frequented was Nussdorf on the Danube. The composer was there in the summer of 1817.

From Beethoven's conversation books:

[April 1826]
Christoph Kuffner: Do you still remember the 'Fischerhaus' near Nussdorf where we sat on the terrace in the light of the full moon until close on to midnight, with the wind in the meadows and the swollen Danube before us? I was your guest there too. –
Kerst II, 296.

98 A view near Mödling; coloured engraving by L. Janscha from a drawing by J. Ziegler, *c.* 1800. Beethoven often spent the summer months in Baden or Mödling when he was not at one of the Bohemian spas.

99 Danube landscape, seen from Nussdorf; anonymous watercolour, end eighteenth century. In June 1817 Beethoven moved to this village, keeping his flat in town.

Letter from Beethoven to Nanette Streicher:

Nussdorf, 7 July [1817]

My dear friend!
I received your letter here, confirming your bad fall. I hope it will improve soon; warm, tepid baths heal all hurts. – The bad weather the day before yesterday kept me from coming to see you when I was in town. Yesterday morning I hurried back here, but did not find my servant at home; he had even taken the keys to my lodgings with him. It was quite chilly and I had come out from town with nothing but a very thin pair of breeches and was forced to loaf about for three hours. This was injurious for me and put me in a foul humour for the whole day. – There you see what happens to households that depend on servants! . . .

Beethovens Briefe, ed. Albert Leitzmann, Leipzig 1912, p. 133. Anderson 785. (Nanette Streicher was the daughter of the piano manufacturer Johann Andreas Stein. She carried on her father's firm.)

Louis Schlösser writes about Beethoven's method of composition (1822/23):

'I carry my ideas about with me for a long time, and often for a very long time, before I write them down,' he [Beethoven] answered. 'In doing so, my memory is so trustworthy that I am sure I will not forget, even after a period of years, a theme I have once committed to memory. I change a great deal, eliminate much and begin again, until I am satisfied with the result; then the working-out, in extension, in diminution, in height and in depth begins in my head, and, since I know what I want, the basic idea never leaves me, it mounts and grows, I hear and see the work in my mind in its full proportions, as though already accomplished, and all that remains is the labour of writing it out; this proceeds quickly, depending on the time I have available, since I often have several pieces in the works at once; I am certain, however, not to confuse one with the other. You will ask me where I get my ideas. That I cannot say with certainty. They come unbidden, indirectly, directly. I could grasp them with my hands; in the midst of nature, in the woods, on walks, in the silence of the night, in the early morning, inspired by moods that translate themselves into words for the poet and into tones for me, that sound, surge, roar, until at last they stand before me as notes.'   Kerst II, 15 f.   *Hallelujah* 4th year, No. 20, 1885.

Anton Schindler on Schimon's painting of Beethoven:

. . . It is worth taking the space to report on the conditions under which this painting was done. At my intercession the artist, who was still quite young, received permission to set up his easel next to the master's workroom, and to work as he saw fit. Beethoven steadfastly refused to grant a sitting, for he was completely engrossed in work on the *Missa Solemnis* and declared that he could not spare a single hour. Schimon, however, had already secretly followed Beethoven's every footstep and had several studies for the painting in his portfolio, and was thus quite satisfied with the permission as granted. When the picture has been completed except for one significant detail, the expression of the eyes, the critical situation arose as to how to achieve this most difficult end; for the play of the eyes in Beethoven's head was of a singular nature, revealing a gamut of expressions, ranging from the wildest and most defiant to the gentlest and most affectionate, equal to the gamut of his emotions. For a painter this was, then, the most difficult obstacle. The master himself helped to overcome it. The uncouth, blunt nature of the young painter, his unceremonious behaviour as though he were in his own studio, his habit of arriving without saying 'Good morning' and leaving without saying 'Goodbye', had attracted Beethoven's attention even more than what stood on the easel; in short, the young man began to interest him. He invited him to coffee. Schimon used the impromptu sitting at the coffee table to work out the eyes. Further invitations to a cup of coffee, at 60 beans per cup, gave the painter the opportunity to finish his work, with which Beethoven was utterly satisfied.   Schindler II, 288 f.

163

Anton Schindler on Beethoven's eyes:

... Rochlitz reports how Beethoven received his suggestion concerning music to *Faust*, in the following words: 'He [Beethoven] read. Ha! he cried, and threw up his hands. That would be a piece of work! Something could come of that! He went on a while in this manner, proceeding forthwith to lay plans in his mind, and not at all badly, all the while staring at the ceiling, his head bent back.'

The latter observation belongs to the afore-mentioned play of the eyes in Beethoven's head. His eyes, which usually appeared to be small, frequently became large and prominent, and their gaze, directed upwards, would remain fixed for some time on the ceiling or on the sky, either in meditation or when something in the conversation had affected him strongly. Only Schimon caught that characteristic completely; Stieler merely hinted at it. The illness Beethoven suffered at the beginning of 1825 had destroyed the brightness of his eyes, so that, as many inward and outward metamorphoses began at that time, nothing more of the curious play of the eyes could be perceived from then onwards. Stieler's painting agrees excellently with that outward change.
Schindler II, 292 f.

Anton Schindler reports on Beethoven's clothing:

In choosing the articles of apparel to appear in the portrait of an historical figure, due consideration has to be given to a number of points; among them is the distinction that has to be made between everyday and festive clothing, and even between good and bad seasons of the year. Still more particular attention will have to be paid to a Beethoven, who knew how to dress decently for the street as well as for the drawing-room. In this regard it must be said of the master that, until the last days of his life, conditions permitting, he was fond of dressing painstakingly and that there was always harmony in his apparel. A frock-coat of fine blue cloth with metal buttons (blue was his favourite colour at that time) suited him excellently. Such a frock-coat, with another of dark green cloth, was never missing from his wardrobe. During the summer one always saw him in fair weather in white trousers, shoes and white stockings (then the fashion). His waistcoat and necktie were white at every season and were conspicuous for their exemplary cleanliness even on weekdays. Apart from this attire one must imagine a light step and an erect carriage, light movements in general, which were always characteristic of Beethoven, and one will have Beethoven's personality before one.
Schindler II, 294 f.

*Carl Friedrich Hirsch describes Beethoven's appearance, as taken down by
Theodor von Frimmel:*

Hirsch confirmed what was said about the musical Titan's powerful
build and the healthy ruddy colouring of his face; Hirsch, too, drew
my attention to the fact that Beethoven's eyebrows were quite bushy
and his forehead low (a statement confirmed by the skull and the
existing masks, but contradicted by less credible assertions about a high
forehead which have come from various scattered quarters). The nose,
Hirsch says, was large and broad, particularly the nostrils (which were
always soundly 'worked over'). Beethoven's hair was quite thick, bushy
and dark – though mixed with grey – and stood up from his forehead.
Now and then, when reading music, the master used eyeglasses, but
he did not wear them constantly. – On this occasion I showed Herr
Hirsch my collection of Beethoven portraits, to ask him which were
good likenesses and which were not. He found that a small medallion
in my possession, showing the head turned to the right, was the most
similar; it was done from life by a renowned old Viennese artist at the
beginning of the 1820s. The artist in question is Josef Daniel Böhm
(1794–1865). Of the other Beethoven portraits I showed him, Hirsch
described the one made after the Schimon portrait as good. In most of
the others he found the forehead too high. Of the later ones, he approved
of those which retained the Schimon or Waldmüller type, among them
the medallion by Brehmer, on which, however, the forehead was also
much too high. The wrinkles in the forehead falling to the bridge of the
nose, as shown in the Stieler portrait, he considered especially true to life.

Beethoven's lack of order at home was also confirmed. Beethoven
worked in a flowered cloth dressing-gown; when not at home he was
to be seen in a dark green or brown coat and grey or black trousers. – In
his room the greatest disorder reigned; music, manuscripts, books lay
around, some on the writing desk, some on the floor. The revered head
was covered by a sort of low top hat or, during the warmer seasons, a
brown or dirty yellow straw hat. His service was seen to by a hotel.

Neue Zeitschrift für Musik, No. 35, 1880. (As a child, Hirsch had had piano lessons from
Beethoven.)

This was the period of the tremendous *Missa Solemnis*, Op. 123, for Archduke
Rudolph. It was Beethoven's faithful copyist, Schlemmer, who prepared the
beautiful score given to the Archduke himself, which is now in the Gesellschaft der
Musikfreunde.

Anton Schindler on the Missa Solemnis:

Towards the end of August [1819] I arrived at the house in Mödling where Beethoven was staying; with me was Johann Horzalka, a musician who is still living in Vienna. It was four in the afternoon. We had no sooner walked in when we were told that Beethoven's two maid-servants had taken themselves off that same morning, and that all the occupants of the house had been disturbed by a scene which took place after midnight, because both servants had fallen asleep after waiting so long and the food they had prepared had turned inedible. In one of the living-rooms, behind closed doors, we heard the master singing, howling and stamping his foot over the *Credo* fugue. We had listened for some time to the awful scene and were about to leave, when the door opened and Beethoven stood facing us with features so distorted as to fill one with alarm. He looked as though he had just survived a life-and-death battle with the whole host of contrapuntalists, his perpetual opponents. His first remarks were confused, as though he were unpleasantly surprised at our eavesdropping. But he presently came to speak of the issues of the day and remarked with perceptible composure, 'A fine business. Everyone has run off and I have had nothing to eat since yesterday noon.' I sought to mollify him and helped him to dress. My companion hurried on ahead to the dining-room at the baths to have something prepared for our famished master. There he complained to us about the bad conditions of his household. For various reasons there was no remedying them. Surely no work of art of such magnitude has ever been created in more unpleasant living conditions than was the *Missa Solemnis*!

Schindler I, 270 f.

Friedrich Johann Rochlitz describes Beethoven to his wife (1822):

Imagine a man of about fifty, of less than medium height, but of quite powerful, stocky build; thick-set, and in particular of strong bone structure – somewhat like Fichte, but more fleshy, especially the face, which is fuller and rounder; a red, healthy colour; restless, bright eyes, almost piercing when they gaze steadily; no movements, or else quick ones; in the expression of the countenance, particularly of the intelligent and lively eyes, a mixture or at times an instantaneous alternation of the most cordial good nature and shyness; in his whole attitude the tension, the uneasy, anxious listening of a deaf man who is highly sensitive; now a word thrown out happily and freely, followed by an immediate plunge into gloomy silence; added to all that, the feelings of the observer which

100 Autograph page of Piano Sonata in C Minor, Op. 111, written in 1822 and dedicated to Archduke Rudolph.

unceasingly make themselves heard: this is the man who brings pure joy to millions – pure spiritual joy! – He said some friendly and cordial things to me in broken sentences; I raised my voice when I could, spoke slowly, accentuated carefully, and in the fulness of my heart thanked him for his works, what they mean to me and will mean to me all my life; drew special attention to some of my favourites and elaborated on them; I told him how masterly were the executions of his symphonies in Leipzig and how the public loudly expressed its approval, etc. He stood close to me, sometimes looking intently at my face and sometimes lowering his head; then he smiled, nodded in a friendly way, but said nothing. Had he understood me? Or not? Finally I had to stop; then he shook my hand vigorously and said, rather curtly, to ★ ★ ★ [Carl, the nephew?]: 'I have some things to do.' And to me, as he left, 'We shall see each other again.' ★ ★ ★ accompanied him out of the house. I was deeply moved and disturbed. Then ★ ★ ★ came back. 'Did he understand me?' I asked. ★ ★ ★ shrugged his shoulders: 'Not a word.' We were silent a long while, and I cannot express how moved I was. Finally I asked: 'Why didn't you repeat at least some of it, since he seems to understand you?' 'I didn't want to interrupt you and he's very touchy. But I'd hoped, really, that he would have understood some of it: however, the noises from the street, your speech (which he isn't used to), and perhaps even his haste to try to understand everything – because he probably saw that you were saying nice things to him – He was so sad.'

I cannot describe the mood in which I left. The same man, who delights all the world with the beauty of his tones, can hear none, not even the tones of him who wants to express his gratefulness; even more, it becomes a torment for him! . . . Roughly a fortnight later I was just on my way to lunch when I met the young composer Franz Schubert, an ardent admirer of Beethoven. He had spoken to him about me. 'If you want to see him merry and less self-conscious,' Schubert said, 'then you should lunch now at the inn where he has just gone.' – He took me there. Most of the tables were occupied. Beethoven sat surrounded by several of his acquaintances, who were strangers to me. He actually did seem merry. He returned my salutation; but I deliberately did not join him. I found a place at a table where I could see him and could make out most of what he said, for he spoke loudly enough. What he carried on was not actually a conversation; he spoke alone, and for the most part rather steadily, as though at random and into the blue. His listeners added little, only laughing or nodding in approbation. He – philosophized, and talked politics in his own way. He spoke of England and the English, he conceived of them as being incomparably excellent – which to some extent sounded quite curious. Then he told stories about the French from the two times they occupied Vienna. He could not stand them at all. He said everything with the greatest carelessness and without the least restraint, but spiced with highly original, naive judgments or droll fancies.

Kerst I, 282 f.   Rochlitz, *op. cit.*, pp. 351 ff.

From Sir George Smart's diary for Sunday, 11 September 1825 [original *English*]:

. . . From hence I went alone to Schlesinger's, at the 'Wildemann', where was a larger party than the previous one. Among them was l'Abbé Stadler, a fine old man and a good composer of the old school, to whom I was introduced. There was also present a pupil of Moscheles, a Mademoiselle Eskeles and a Mademoiselle Cimia, whom I understood to be a professional player. When I entered Messrs. C. Czerny, Schuppanzigh and Lincke had just begun the trio, op. 70 of Beethoven, after this the same performers played Beethoven's trio, op. 97 – both printed singly by Steiner. Then followed Beethoven's quartette, the same that I heard on September the 9th, and it was played by the same performers. Beethoven was seated near the pianoforte beating time during the performance of these pieces. This ended, most of the company departed, but Schlesinger invited me to stop and dine with the following party of ten. Beethoven, his nephew, Holz, Weiss, C. Czerny, who sat at the bottom of the table, Lincke, Jean Sedlatzek – a flute player who is coming to England next year, and has letters to the Duke of Devonshire, Count St. Antonio, etc. – he has been to Italy – Schlesinger, Schuppanzigh, who sat at the top, and myself. Beethoven calls Schuppanzigh Sir John Falstaff, not a bad name considering the figure of this excellent violin player.

We had a most pleasant dinner, healths were given in the English style. Beethoven was delightfully gay but hurt that, in the letter Moscheles gave me, his name should be mixed up with the other professors. . . . After dinner he was coaxed to play extempore, observing in French to me, 'Upon what subject shall I play?' Meanwhile he was touching the instrument thus

to which I answered, 'Upon that.' On which theme he played for about twenty minutes in a most extraordinary manner, sometimes very fortissimo, but full of genius. When he rose at the conclusion of his playing he appeared greatly agitated. No one could be more agreeable than he was – plenty of jokes. He was in the highest of spirits. We all wrote to him by turns, but he can hear a little if you halloo quite close to his left ear.

Leaves from the Journals of Sir George Smart, edited by H. Bertram Cox and C. L. E. Cox, London 1907, pp. 113 ff. (Sir George Smart, musician and organist, came to Vienna in 1825, in the course of a European tour, and met Beethoven there.)

By this time, Beethoven was a well-known figure in Vienna. People were used to his rather wild appearance and also proud of his presence in the Royal and Imperial city. Beethoven was often seen walking in the popular Paradeplatz, and there is a detailed description of him at this period by Dr Gerhard von Breuning, son of Stephan, Beethoven's old friend.

101 The *Paradeplatz* (parade square) in front of the Burgtor, Vienna; coloured engraving by L. Beyer, 1805. This was a popular walking spot.

Dr Gerhard von Breuning describes Beethoven's appearance:

Beethoven's outward appearance, due to his quite peculiar nonchalance in the matter of dress, had something uncommonly conspicuous about it in the street. Usually lost in thought and humming to himself, he often gesticulated with his arms when walking by himself. When in company, he would speak quite animatedly and loudly, and, since his companion then had to write his rejoinder in the conversation book, an abrupt halt would have to be made; this was conspicuous in itself, and was still more so when the rejoinder was communicated in mime.

And so it happened that most of the passers-by would turn around to stare at him; the street urchins also made their gibes and shouted after him. For that reason his nephew Carl refused to go out with him and once told him straight out that he was ashamed to accompany him in the street because of his 'comical appearance'; at this, so he told us, he was greatly insulted and hurt. For my part, I was proud to be able to show myself with a man of his importance.

The crown of the felt hat he wore at that time had lost its shape and bulged towards the top where it had been stretched; this was the result of Beethoven's habit, on coming in, of clapping his hat over the topmost point of the hall-stand; should the hat be dripping with rain, he would simply shake it lightly first, which he also did at our house without a thought for the furniture. The hat was rarely if ever brushed, either before or after rain, and, becoming increasingly dusty, it took on a permanently matted appearance. He wore it, when feasible, at the back of his head to have his forehead free, while his grey, unkempt hair (in Rellstab's apt words, 'not frizzly, not straight, but a mixture of everything') flew out on both sides. By wearing the hat far out of the face and tilting it towards the back while keeping his head erect, the rear part of the brim collided with the collar of the coat, which at that time was worn quite high; this gave the brim a turned-up shape, while the collar, due to constant contact with the hat-brim, appeared to have been rubbed threadbare. The lapels of the coat (especially those of the blue frock-coat with brass buttons) were not fastened, and flapped back against his arms, particularly when he walked into the wind; the two long points of the neck-cloth, which was knotted about the wide shirt-collar, likewise flew outwards. The double lorgnette, which he wore for his nearsightedness, hung loose. The coat-tails were rather heavily laden: apart from a pocket handkerchief, which often showed, they contained a quite thick, folded, quarto music notebook and an octavo conversation book with a thick carpenter's pencil,* for communicating with friends and acquaintances he might happen to meet; and at an earlier period, so long as it was of any use, an ear-trumpet. The weight of the music notebook lengthened the one coat-tail considerably, and the pocket was often turned inside out when the notebook and conversation book were extracted from it. . . . I often saw him thus from our windows, when I was not with him myself, coming at about two o'clock – his dinner hour – from the Schottentor across the part of the Glacis where the Votivkirche now stands, sailing towards his lodgings in his customary posture, his body leant forward (but not bowed), his head erect.

Breuning 96 ff. (Footnote in the original text.)

Ferdinand Ries on Beethoven's irritability:

Beethoven was sometimes extremely violent. One day we were dining at the Swan; the waiter brought him the wrong dish. Beethoven had scarcely said a few choice words about it, which the waiter had answered perhaps not quite so politely as he should have, when Beethoven laid hold of the dish (it was a so-called 'Lungenbratel' [a kind of roast-beef]

---

* In the same way that Beethoven was peculiarly awkward when it came to cutting quill pens for himself, his rather clumsy fingers also proved to be ill suited to sharpening pencils without quickly breaking them. This may have been the reason he preferred to procure thick-gauge pencils for himself, similar to those used by carpenters.

with lots of sauce) and flung it at the waiter's head. The poor fellow still had on his arm a large number of plates containing various dishes (a dexterity which Viennese waiters possess to a high degree) and could do nothing to help himself; the sauce ran down his face. He and Beethoven shouted and cursed at each other, while all the other guests laughed out loud. Finally Beethoven began laughing at the sight of the waiter, who lapped up with his tongue the sauce that was running down his face, tried to go on hurling insults, but had to go on lapping instead, pulling the most ludicrous faces the while, a picture worthy of Hogarth. . . .

Beethoven hardly knew what money was, which often gave rise to unpleasant scenes because, mistrustful in general, he often believed he had been cheated when in fact he had not. Quickly aroused, he bluntly called people cheats, which in the case of waiters had to be made good by a tip. Ultimately his peculiarities and his absent-mindedness became so well known at the inns he most frequented, that everything was tolerated, even when he left without paying.
Kerst I, 98.

Carl Czerny writes about Beethoven's reputation in Vienna:

It has sometimes been said abroad that Beethoven was neglected and oppressed in Vienna. The truth is that he enjoyed, even as a young man, all possible support and an encouragement and respect on the part of our high nobility which has rarely been the portion of a young composer.

Later too, when he had alienated many of his well-wishers by his hypochondria, no difficulties were ever put in the way of his often conspicuous idiosyncrasies; this accounts for his preference for Vienna. And it is doubtful whether he would have remained so unchallenged in any other country. It is true that, as an artist, he had to contend with intrigues, but the public had no part in them. He was always esteemed and stared at in wonder as an exceptional being, and his greatness was also sensed by his opponents, who did not understand him. He could have been well off, but he was not made for domestic order.
Czerny 14.

Anton Schindler on Beethoven's daily schedule:

As regards our composer's daily schedule, he customarily arose at dawn at every season of the year and went at once to his writing-desk. He worked until 2 or 3 o'clock, at which hour he ate his dinner. During his working hours he would usually go out of doors once or twice, where he (in Saphir's words) worked while walking. Such excursions seldom

102–106 Contemporary sketches or recollections of Beethoven by Joseph Weidner (*above left*), J. D. Böhm (*above right*), Martin Tejček (*below left*), J. D. Böhm (*below centre*) and J. N. Hoechle (*below right*).

lasted more than an hour and resembled the flights of bees to gather honey; they took place whatever the season, and neither heat nor cold were heeded. The afternoons were kept for regular walks; later he would stop in at a favourite tavern to peruse the daily newspapers, if this need had not already been satisfied at a coffee-house. When the English parliament was in session, however, the *Allgemeine Zeitung* was regularly read at home for its reports of the debates. It will be easily understood that our amateur politician was on the side of the opposition; this would have been so even if he had not been partial to Lord Brougham, Hume and other opposition orators. Beethoven always stayed home on winter's evenings, which were devoted to serious reading. Only rarely did one see him engaged in writing music in the evening, because this was too tiring to his eyes. This might not have been the case when he was younger. It is certain, however, that at no time did he use the evening hours for composition. He went to bed at 10 o'clock at the latest.
Schindler II, 192.

Wilhelmine Schröder-Devrient recalls the rehearsals for Fidelio:

. . . But Beethoven sat before the orchestra, with all the participants depending on his baton, and I had never laid eyes on the man before! – At that time the master's physical ear was already closed to all sounds. Waving his baton to and fro with violent movements, a puzzled expression on his face and celestial inspiration in his eyes, he stood among the playing musicians and did not hear a note! When, in his opinion, a passage was to be played *piano*, he would creep almost under the music-stand, when he wanted *forte* he would leap upwards with the most curious gestures and utter the strangest sounds. With every number our anxiety grew, and it seemed to me that I was watching one of Hoffmann's weird figures emerge before me. It was inevitable that the deaf composer caused the most complete confusion among the singers and orchestra and got everyone quite out of time, so that no one knew any longer where they were. But Beethoven observed nothing of all that, and so we somehow managed to finish the rehearsal, with which he seemed to be quite satisfied, for he laid aside the baton with a cheerful smile. It was unthinkable, however, that he should be entrusted with the performance, and Kapellmeister Umlauf had to take on the heart-breaking task of telling him that the opera could not be put on with him conducting.

174   Kerst II, 39 ff.

Anton Schindler on the 1822 revival of Beethoven's Fidelio:

. . . When I had come up to the orchestra pit [during the rehearsal] and was standing close to him, he handed me his note-book with a sign to write down what was the matter. I quickly wrote more or less these words: 'I beg you not to go on, the rest at home.' In a trice he sprang over the barrier into the stalls and said only, 'Let us go out quickly.' Without stopping, he ran towards his lodgings in the Pfarrgasse in the suburb of Leimgrube. Once inside the door, he threw himself down on the sofa, covered his face with both hands and stayed in that position until we sat down to the table. Nor did he make a sound during the meal; his whole body was a picture of the deepest depression and despondency. When I attempted to go after dinner he asked me not to leave him until time for the performance. . . .
Schindler II, 11.

Louis Schlösser reports on the revival of Fidelio:

Feverishly excited by the marvellous closing hymn, that apotheosis of true conjugal love, I scarcely noticed that the house was gradually emptying, until my faithful friend Franz Schubert took my arm to lead me to the exit. Three gentlemen left, at the same time as we did, from the lower corridor that leads to the boxes. I paid no attention to them, however, for their backs were towards me, but I was amazed to see that everyone leaving made way for them. Schubert plucked at my sleeve and pointed to the man in the middle, who had just turned around; the bright light of the lamps shone on his face, and I recognized the features of the composer of the evening's opera, Beethoven, familiar to me from etchings and portraits. My heart beat deafeningly at that moment, and I do not recall whether I said anything to Schubert, or, if so, what it was. But I do recall that I followed that longed-for figure and his companions (Schindler and Breuning, as I later learned) like a shadow through winding streets, past high-gabled houses, until the darkness of the night hid them from my sight. – –
Kerst II, 4 f.

Anton Schindler on Schubert's visit to Beethoven:

It was a dark day for Franz Schubert when, in 1822, he called on Beethoven to present a copy of the Piano Variations for Four Hands which he had dedicated to the master. Despite the company of Diabelli, who acted as the interpreter of Schubert's sentiments for the master at the meeting, the shy and taciturn young composer played a rôle disagreeable to

175

everyone including himself. His courage, which had held fast as far as the house, deserted him completely at the sight of His Musical Majesty. And when Beethoven expressed the wish that Schubert himself should write down the answers to his questions, the latter's hand seemed to be chained. Beethoven looked through the copy hastily and came across an error in the harmony. He drew the young man's attention to it with kindly words, adding immediately that it was not a mortal sin. Schubert, however, was utterly disconcerted now, perhaps as a result of Beethoven's soothing remark. Not until he had left the house did he pull himself together, and then he cursed himself in the most common terms. He never had the courage to try to make the master's acquaintance again.

Schindler II, 176.

Anton Schindler describes the relationship between Beethoven and Schubert:

Since the illness, to which Beethoven finally succumbed after four months' suffering, made his customary artistic activity impossible from the time it began, we had to think of some diversion for him in keeping with his intellect and his interests. And so it happened that I showed him a collection of Schubert's songs, about 60 in number, many of which were then still in manuscript. It was not my sole purpose to provide him with pleasant entertainment, but rather to give him the opportunity of becoming acquainted with the real Schubert, of forming a favourable opinion of his talent, which had been made suspect for him by those exalted beings who have doubtless done the same for others of their contemporaries. The great master, who until that time had known less than half a dozen of Schubert's songs, was astonished at their number and could not be made to believe that Schubert had by then [February 1827] already written more than five hundred. But if he was astounded at the number, he was even more amazed when he came to know their content. For several days he could hardly put them down, and every day he spent hours at a time with Iphigenia's monologue, the *Grenzen der Menschheit, Allmacht*, the *Young Nun, Viola*, the *Müllerlieder* and others. Again and again he cried out enthusiastically, 'Truly, there is a divine spark in Schubert!' – 'If I had had this poem I would have set it to music too!' he said of most of the poems, the subject and content of which, together with Schubert's original setting, he could not praise enough. . . . In short, Beethoven gained such great respect for Schubert's talent that he now wanted to see his operas and piano pieces too; but his illness had advanced to the point where he could no longer satisfy that desire. But

he spoke often of Schubert, prophesying that 'he will cause a stir in the world,' and regretting that he had not come to know him earlier.
Kerst I, 274 f.

Letter from Anselm Hüttenbrenner to Professor Luib:

I know for certain that Professor Schindler, Schubert and I paid a visit to Beethoven's bedside roughly a week before he died. Schindler announced us both and asked Beethoven which one of us he wished to see first. Beethoven answered, 'Let Schubert come in first.'
Kerst I, 276.   TDR V, 480.

Anton Schindler on Beethoven and the painter Waldmüller:

. . . In early 1823 the publishers Breitkopf & Härtel wanted a portrait of our composer, and Waldmüller, a professor at the Academy, was chosen to do it. There were unfavourable portents to this plan: urgent work to be finished and persistent eye trouble, and ill-humour in consequence. After a long delay, the first sitting was at last arranged. Waldmüller conducted himself deferentially and much too timidly, a demeanour which, with Beethoven, usually led to no success whatever. We have only just heard in what utterly different ways the two painters mentioned previously [Stieler and Schimon] achieved their purpose. Even though Waldmüller made great haste in sketching the head and in roughing, the master, who was deep in thought, found he was taking too long; he left his seat now and again, pacing sulkily up and down the room or going to his writing-desk in the next room. The roughing was not yet finished when Beethoven made it plain that he could bear it no longer. When the painter had left, Beethoven's anger erupted and Waldmüller was called the most miserable of daubers – because he had made him sit facing the window. He stubbornly refused to admit any argument in defence. There were no more sittings. The painter finished the portrait from his imagination, because, as he replied to my remonstrances, he could not do without the contracted fee of 20 ducats. . . .
Schindler II, 290 f. (Waldmüller received only 12 ducats.)

John Russell about Beethoven [original English]:

Beethoven is the most celebrated of the living composers in Vienna, and, in certain departments, the foremost of his day. Though not an old man, he is lost to society in consequence of his extreme deafness, which has rendered him almost unsocial. The neglect of his person which he exhibits gives him a somewhat wild appearance. His features are strong

177

and prominent; his eye is full of rude energy; his hair, which neither comb nor scissors seem to have visited for years, overshadows his broad brow in a quantity and confusion to which only the snakes round a Gorgon's head offer a parallel. His general behaviour does not ill accord with the unpromising exterior. Except when he is among his chosen friends, kindliness or affability are not his characteristics. The total loss of hearing has deprived him of all the pleasure which society can give and perhaps soured his temper. He used to frequent a particular cellar, where he spent the evening in a corner, beyond the reach of all the chattering and disputation of a public room, drinking wine and beer, eating cheese and red herrings, and studying the newspapers. One evening a person took a seat near him whose countenance did not please him. He looked hard at the stranger, and spat on the floor as if he had seen a toad, then glanced at the newspaper, then again at the intruder, and spat again, his hair bristling gradually into more shaggy ferocity, till he closed the alternation of spitting and staring, by fairly exclaiming, 'What a scoundrelly phiz!' and rushing out of the room. Even among his oldest friends he must be humoured like a wayward child. He has always a small paperbook with him, and what conversation takes place is carried on in writing. In this, too, although it is not lined, he instantly jots down any musical idea which strikes him. These notes would be utterly unintelligible even to another musician, for they have thus no comparative value; he alone has in his own mind the thread by which he brings out of this labyrinth of dots and circles the richest and most astounding harmonies. The moment he is seated at the piano, he is evidently unconscious that there is any thing in existence but himself and his instrument; and, considering how very deaf he is, it seems impossible that he should hear all he plays. Accordingly, when playing very *piano*, he often does not bring out a single note. He hears it himself in the 'mind's ear'. While his eye, and the almost imperceptible motion of his fingers, show that he is following out the strain in his own soul through all its dying gradations, the instrument is actually as dumb as the musician is deaf.

I have heard him play, but to bring him so far required some management, so great is his horror of being any thing like exhibited. Had he been plainly asked to do the company that favour, he would have flatly refused; he had to be cheated into it. Every person left the room, except Beethoven and the master of the house, one of his most intimate acquaintances. These two carried on a conversation in the paperbook about bank stock. The gentleman, as if by chance, struck the keys of the open piano, beside which they were sitting, gradually began to run over one of Beethoven's own compositions, made a thousand errors, and speedily blundered one passage so thoroughly, that the composer condescended to stretch out his hand and put him right. It was enough; the hand was on the piano; his companion immediately left him, on some pretext, and joined the rest of the company, who, in the next room, from which they could see and hear every thing, were patiently waiting the issue of this tiresome conjuration. Beethoven, left alone, seated himself at the piano. At first he only struck now and then a few hurried and interrupted notes, as if afraid of being detected in a crime; but gradually he forgot every thing else, and ran on during half an hour in a phantasy, in a style extremely varied, and marked, above all, by the most abrupt transitions. The amateurs were enraptured; to the uninitiated it was more interesting, to observe how the music of the man's soul passed over his countenance. He seems to feel the bold, the commanding, and the impetuous, more than what is soothing or gentle. The muscles of his face swell, and its veins start out; the wild eye rolls doubly wild; the mouth quivers, and Beethoven looks like a wizard, overpowered by the demons whom he himself has called up.

John Russell, *A Tour in Germany and some of the Southern Provinces of the Austrian Empire, in the Years 1820, 1821, 1822*, 2 vols., 3rd edition, Edinburgh 1825, II, 273 ff.

We have to thank Nikolai Borissovich, Prince Galitzin, for the late Quartets that are among the very greatest creations in all music. It is generally asserted that they were not understood when they were first performed in Vienna, but as the documents show this is again one of the half-truths that seem to bedevil Beethoven biographies. This is also the period of the 'Diabelli Variations', Op. 120, which carried to new heights the art of piano variations which Beethoven had so assiduously cultivated throughout his life.

Dr Gerhard von Breuning visits Beethoven:

Once, as often happened, I found him sleeping when I came. I sat down quietly next to his bed so as not to wake him from what I hoped would be an invigorating sleep, and in the meantime leafed through the conversation books lying ready for use on the bedside table, to find out who had been there since my last visit and what had been discussed. I found, among other things, the note: 'Your quartet that Schuppanzigh played yesterday was not well received.' After a short time he awoke, and I showed him that comment, asking him what he had to say about it. 'They will like it, one of these days' was the laconic reply, and he deliberately added curt remarks to the effect that he writes what he

107 Nikolai Borissovich Prince Galitzin; lithograph by G.C. Hahn and F.S. Hanfstaengl. Galitzin, a gifted amateur cellist, was responsible for the first complete performance of the *Missa Solemnis*, which took place at St Petersburg in April 1824.

considers good and does not allow himself to be influenced by the judgment of the day. 'I know, I am a musician.' –
Breuning 142 f.

Carl Holz tells Ludwig Nohl about Beethoven composing the late Quartets:

While composing the three quartets requested by Prince Galitzin, such a wealth of new quartet ideas flowed from Beethoven's inexhaustible imagination that he virtually had to write the Quartets in C-Sharp Minor and F Major involuntarily. 'My dear fellow, I've just had another idea,' he would say jocularly and with glistening eyes when we were out walking, and would write down a few notes in his sketchbook. – –
Kerst II, 187 f.

Apart from the unbelievably rich list of late Quartets, the *Missa Solemnis*, the last Piano Sonatas and the Diabelli Variations, Beethoven was also working on the Ninth Symphony, which he dedicated to the King of Prussia. The documents show how Vienna came to have the world première of the Ninth Symphony and parts of the *Missa Solemnis*. There was a plan afoot to lure Beethoven to Berlin and to have these works performed for the first time in the Prussian capital. As had happened in 1809 when Jerome Bonaparte threatened to take Beethoven away from Vienna, the composer's Viennese friends, appalled at the idea that these great works should be first performed elsewhere, banded together and submitted a petition to the composer, asking him to give Vienna the honour of these new masterpieces. The concert of 7 May 1824, which was repeated, was a financial disaster for Beethoven, although the Ninth Symphony was an enormous success. We know from the conversation books and from other sources that the Viennese broke into applause at the timpani solo in the Scherzo. Among the solo singers were Henriette Sontag and Caroline Unger, attractive young girls who often visited Beethoven during the preparation of the Ninth Symphony.

The violinist Joseph Böhm on the first performance of the Ninth :

The work was studied with the diligence and conscientiousness that such a huge and difficult piece of music demanded. It came to the performance. An illustrious, extremely large audience listened with rapt attention and did not stint with enthusiastic, thundering applause. Beethoven himself conducted, that is, he stood in front of a conductor's stand and threw himself back and forth like a madman. At one moment he stretched to his full height, at the next he crouched down to the floor, he flailed about with his hands and feet as though he wanted to play all the instruments and sing all the chorus parts. – The actual direction was in Duport's hands; we musicians followed his baton only. – Beethoven was so excited that he saw nothing that was going on about him, he paid no heed whatever to the bursts of applause, which his deafness prevented him from hearing in any case. – He had always to be told when it was time to acknowledge the applause, which he did in the most ungracious manner imaginable.

Kerst II, 73. TDR V, 93.

From the Diary of Joseph Carl Rosenbaum :

Friday, 7 [May 1824]. Warm . . . At the K. Th. van Bethowen's concert, with Sontag, Unger, Heitzinger and Seipelt singing, Umlauf conducting. He sympathizes with it. Overture and three Hymns with Kyrie and Ode to Joy; lovely but tedious – not very full – . . . to the K. Th. Many boxes empty, no one from the Court. For all the large forces, little effect. B.'s disciples clamoured, most of the audience stayed quiet, many did not wait for the end. –

Autograph, Österreichische Nationalbibliothek, Handschriftensammlung.

Leopold Sonnleithner reports on the performance of the Ninth Symphony *in the* Allgemeine Musikalische Zeitung, *No. 14, 6 April 1864 :*

You ask me to inform you on the basis of my personal recollection, about the tempo Beethoven took in the double-bass recitatives in the last movement of his Ninth Symphony. I do not hesitate to comply with that request, and state first of all that in the spring of 1824 I attended all (or most) of the orchestral rehearsals of the Ninth Symphony, which was performed for the first time on 7 May 1824. Beethoven himself stood at the head of the forces, but the actual conducting of the orchestra was looked after by Umlauf, who beat time, and Schuppanzigh as first violin. – I can confirm from my own experience that Beethoven had the recitatives played quickly, that is, not exactly *presto* but not *andante* either. The whole symphony, especially the last movement, caused great difficulty for the orchestra, which did not understand it at first, although leading musicians (such as Mayseder, Böhm, Jansa, Linke) were playing in it. The double-bass players had not the faintest idea what they were supposed to do with the recitatives. One heard nothing but a gruff rumbling in the basses, almost as though the composer had intended to offer practical evidence that instrumental music is absolutely incapable of speech. The more often this gigantic work was performed subsequently, the better the musicians and the audience came to terms with it. – . . .

On this occasion I cannot refrain from mentioning something my deceased friend Carl Czerny (a favourite pupil of Beethoven's) repeatedly related to me and which he confirmed as being reliably true. Some time after the first performance of the Ninth Symphony, Beethoven is supposed to have announced to a small group of his closest friends, among them Czerny, that he realized he had committed a blunder with the last movement of the symphony; he wanted, therefore, to eliminate it and write an instrumental movement without voices in its place; he already had an idea in mind for it.

Although the less favourable reception of the final movement with chorus was probably not entirely without influence on this statement of Beethoven's, he was certainly not the man to waver in his views as a result of criticisms of the day or less than customary applause. Therefore, it seems in fact that he did not feel quite comfortable on the new path he had taken. In any event it is greatly to be regretted that his announced intention was never carried out.

Kerst II, 78 f.

Joseph Hüttenbrenner tells how Beethoven who had expected a large profit from the concert on 7 May 1824, took the news that only 420 Gulden had been realized:

I handed him the ticket-office figures. He collapsed at the sight of them. We picked him up and laid him on the sofa. We stayed at his side until late at night; he did not ask for food or anything else, and did not speak.

108 Beethoven; chalk drawing by Stephan Decker, May 1824. Beethoven may have been liverish when the drawing was done, for he looks rather thin and the round cheeks of earlier times are somewhat sunken.

Finally, on perceiving that Morpheus had gently closed his eyes, we went away. His servants found him the next morning as we had left him, asleep and still in the clothes in which he had conducted.
Kerst II, 79.

Anton Schindler describes Beethoven's mistrustfulness:

Beethoven believed that he owed Umlauf, Schuppanzigh and me some thanks for our efforts. A few days after the second academy, therefore, he ordered a meal at the *Wilder Mann* in the Prater. He arrived in the company of his nephew, his brow hung round with dark clouds, acted coldly, using a biting, carping tone in everything he said. An explosion was to be expected. We had only just sat down at the table when he brought the conversation round to the subject of the pecuniary result of the first performance in the theatre, blurting out point-blank that he had been defrauded by the administrator Duport and me together. Umlauf and Schuppanzigh made every effort to prove the impossibility of a fraud of any sort, pointing out that every piece of money had passed through the hands of the two theatre cashiers, that the figures tallied

183

precisely, and that furthermore his nephew, on the instructions of his apothecary brother, had superintended the cashiers in defiance of all custom. Beethoven, however, persisted in his accusation, adding that he had been informed of the fraud from a reliable quarter. Now it was time to give satisfaction for this affront. I went off quickly with Umlauf, and Schuppanzigh, after having to endure several volleys at his voluminous person, soon followed. We gathered at the *Goldenes Lamm* in the Leopoldstadt to continue our interrupted meal undisturbed. The furious composer, however, was left to vent his anger at the waiters and the trees, and as punishment had to eat the opulent meal alone with his nephew.

Schindler II, 88.

Felix von Weingartner writes in his book Akkorde:

Frau Grebner told me and several other devout listeners that she had taken part in the first performance as a soprano in the chorus. Beethoven sat among the performers from the first rehearsal onwards, to be able to hear as much as his condition would permit. He had a stand in front of him, on which his manuscript lay. The young girl, who now sat before me as a venerable old lady, stood just a few steps away from that stand and thus had Beethoven constantly in view. Her description of him is the same as the one that has been handed down to us: a thick-set, very robust, somewhat corpulent man, with a ruddy, pock-marked face and dark, piercing eyes. His grey hair often fell in thick strands over his forehead. His voice, she said, was a sonorous bass; he spoke little, however, for the most part reading pensively in his score. One had the tragic impression that he was incapable of following the music. Although he appeared to be reading along, he would continue to turn pages when the movement in question had already come to an end. At the performance a man went up to him at the end of each movement, tapped him on the shoulder and pointed to the audience. The motion of the clapping hands and the waving handkerchiefs caused him to bow, which always gave rise to great jubilation. Altogether, the effect made by the work at its first performance was quite prodigious. At times there was a burst of applause during a movement. One such moment, Frau Grebner recalled, was the unexpected entrance of the timpani in the Scherzo.

This had the effect of a bolt of lightning and produced a spontaneous show of enthusiasm. Anyone who knows the Viennese public will not be surprised.

Kerst II, 80f. F. von Weingartner, *Akkorde*, Leipzig 1912, p. 1 f.

From Beethoven's conversation books about the second concert, 23 May:

[May 1824]

[Carl:] It was not full, because many people are already in the country. – Some stayed away because they were disgusted about the Rossini aria, as was I.

I was in the auditorium to hear the comments too. Everyone was infuriated at the aria. Stadler had a small group about him who poked fun at it. It cannot harm you, only insofar as people may dwell on the thought that your compositions are desecrated by being, as it were, put into the same category as Rossini's strummings.

Kerst I, 293. (At the second concert an aria by Rossini was put on the programme between Beethoven's Mass and the Ninth Symphony.)

Anton Schindler on Beethoven's relations with the Viennese musical élite:

The year 1823 witnessed the reawakening of a frenzy for Italian opera which degenerated into a veritable Italian *fanatismo* ... two years later this state of affairs had reached such a pitch of depravity that the *Allgemeine Musikalische Zeitung* published the following item from Vienna: 'For years now hardly a single significant interesting piece of music has been published in Vienna; nothing but pianoforte arrangements of Rossini's operas. All is barren. Whither next?'

The depressing character of this period must form the predicate for the events we are about to discuss if we are to achieve a correct understanding of them. It is not difficult to imagine how hard-hit our sublime master was by these conditions. The *Missa Solemnis* had been completed two years earlier, and the Ninth Symphony was finished except for the last touches. How was a performance of the two works to be brought about, with prospects of artistic as well as financial success (the latter taking into account the costs of mounting the performance), in the presence of such general depravity? Therefore, Beethoven had taken advantage of his correspondence with Count Brühl to ask whether a performance of the two works in Berlin could be arranged under his auspices. Count Brühl encouraged the master to proceed on that assumption and promised a successful outcome. When this became known in Vienna, a small group of musicians and music-lovers, who still retained a genuine and sober-minded interest in their art, was moved to band together for the purpose of averting the disgrace threatening the imperial city. An address to the master was drafted and a deputation of the élite presented it to him. It follows verbatim:

185

To Herr Ludwig van Beethoven.

'A small group of disciples and lovers of the arts steps forward today from the large circle of respectful admirers surrounding your genius in its second native city, to express desires long cherished, to give modest voice to requests long restrained.

'The spokesmen are few in number when compared to the company of those who recognize your worth with rejoicing and who are conscious of what you have come to mean to times present and future; and those desires and requests are by no means limited to the spokesmen representing so many like-minded persons. We may affirm in the name of all those to whom art and the realization of their ideals are more than means and objects of amusement, that our desires are the desires of countless people, that our requests are repeated, aloud and silently, by everyone whose breast is stirred by the awareness of the divine in music.

'We express in particular the desires of the music-lovers of our own nation, for although Beethoven's name and works belong to the age and to every land in which sensitive minds are receptive to art, Austria may still claim him for its own at present. Its inhabitants have not yet lost their appreciation of the great and immortal works created for all time by Mozart and Haydn in the bosom of their homeland, and they are conscious, with joyful pride, that the sacred trinity in which those names and yours shine as the symbol of the sublime in the realm of harmony, has sprung fron native soil.

'Thus it is all the more painful for us to be forced to watch an alien influence invade the citadel of that musical nobility; to see figures that can claim no relationship to the princely spirits of that dynasty lead a dance of victory over the burial mounds of the deceased and about the abode of the one man of that trinity who is left to us; to see inanity abuse the name and insignia of art; to watch the understanding for the pure and the eternally beautiful darken and vanish in unseemly dalliance with a sacred art.

'We therefore feel more strongly than ever that one thing is needed precisely at this moment: a revival led by a strong hand, a reappearance of the monarch of his realm. This need brings us to you today, and the following are the requests we address to you for all those by whom these desires are cherished, and in the name of the art of their homeland.

'Withhold no longer from the public, deny no longer to the suffering sense of greatness and consummateness, the performance of the latest masterpieces from your hand. We know that a large sacred composition has followed that first such work in which you immortalized the feelings of a soul pervaded and transfigured by the power of faith and celestial light. We know that in the garden of your glorious and unexcelled symphonies a new blossom glows. For years, since the thunder of the Battle of Vittoria died away, we have waited and hoped to witness the bestowal, within the circle of your own disciples, of new gifts from the abundance of your riches. Disappoint our expectations no longer! Deepen the impression of your newest works by allowing us the pleasure of making their acquaintance through yourself! Do not permit your most recent children to be introduced to their birthplace perhaps as foreigners, by people to whom you and your spirit are alien! Appear soon among your friends, your admirers and venerators! – This is our first and foremost request.

'But other demands upon your genius have become audible too. The desires and offers addressed to you more than one year ago by the directors of the Court Opera and somewhat thereafter by the Society of Austrian Friends of Music, were too long the silent desires of all venerators of music and your name, and raised too many hopes and expectations, not to have found the swiftest dissemination near and far, not to have awakened the most universal interest. – Poetry has done its part to give support to such great hopes and desires. A worthy subject, from the hand of an esteemed poet, waits for your imagination to call it to life. Do not let that fervent summons to so noble a goal remain unheard! Delay no longer in reconveying to us those vanished days when Polyhymnia's song moved and delighted the initiates of art and the heart of the masses in equal measure!

'Should we tell you with what deep regret your seclusion has long been felt? Must we assure you that, as all eyes were turned hopefully towards you, we were aggrieved to see the man we regard as the first among the living in his realm watch silently as foreign art encamps on German soil and sits in the place of honour of the German muse; as German works degenerate into mere echoes of foreign tunes, and a dotage of taste threatens to follow the golden age of art.

'Only you can secure victory for the efforts of the best of us. The musical societies of the fatherland and the German opera await a new efflorescence, a regeneration and a new reign of the true and the beautiful over the foreign power to which the fashion of the day seeks to subjugate the eternal precepts of art. Give us the hope that the desires of all those people who have been reached by the sounds of your harmonies may soon be fulfilled. This is our second most earnest request. – May the year now beginning not come to a close without gratifying us with the fruits of our requests; may the coming spring bring one of the desired gifts with it, and so become a twofold time of efflorescence for us and for the whole world of art.'

Vienna, February 1824.

Signed:

Prince C. Lichnowsky.	Ferd. Count Palfy	M. Count Dietrichstein.
Artaria und Comp.	Ed. Frh. v. Schweiger.	Ig. Edler von Mosel,
v. Hauschka.	Count Czernin,	I. & R. Hofrat.
	Chamberlain.	
M. J. Leidesdorf.	Moritz Count Fries.	Karl Czerny.
J. E. von Wayna.	I. F. Castelli.	M. Count Lichnowsky.
Andreas Streicher.	Prof. Deinhardtstein.	v. Zmeskall.
Anton Halm.	Ch. Kuffner.	Hofrat Kiesewetter.
Abbé Stadler.	F. R. Nehammer, perm.	L. Sonnleithner, Dr.
von Felsburg, Court Sec'y.	Sec'y.	Steiner und Comp.
Ferd. Count Stockhammer.	Steiner von Felsburg,	Lederer.
Anton Diabelli.	Banker.	J. N. Bihler.

It had been expected that Beethoven would read the address in the presence of Court Secretary von Felsburg and J. N. Bihler, the two signatories delegated to hand it to him; this would give them a chance to discuss various other points and to obtain a definite promise from him. The hour after dinner was chosen for the presentation of the paper, for at that time the master was usually accessible for an extended conversation. The deputies erred, however. Beethoven wanted to read the document later, when he would be alone. It may be taken for granted that he was not a little surprised at receiving it, especially since his trust in everyone's attitude towards him was already quite shaken and his trust in the corps of musicians was completely non-existent; he had spoken his mind about that to Court Councillor Rochlitz in 1822 in no uncertain terms, . . . It may be guessed to what extent I, for my part, was interested in the impression the address would make. I could not refrain from calling on the master immediately after it was presented. I found him with the paper in his hand. After he had told me what had just happened, he handed me the page with a composure that showed only too clearly how moved he was by its contents. While I read what I already knew, he went to the window and looked at the clouds floating past. I put the paper aside without speaking, waiting for him to begin. He remained in the position I have described. Finally he turned to me and spoke in a curiously high-pitched tone: 'It is really very nice! – I am happy about it!' This was the cue for me to express my happiness

109 Autograph page of the Cavatina from the String Quartet, Op. 130, the third of three works commissioned by Prince Galitzin. A substitute final movement finished towards the end of 1826 was Beethoven's last completed work.

too – unfortunately in writing. He read it and said quickly, 'Let us go out!' Out of doors he remained monosyllabic in contrast to his customary behaviour, again an unmistakable sign of what was going on in his soul. Schindler II, 59 ff.

The new Quartets were now being played in Vienna. We have various and interesting eye-witness reports, among others from Carl Holz, who was at this time Beethoven's amanuensis, taking the place of Schindler. Schindler loathed Holz and has given us a very warped view of him and his relations with Beethoven. Holz left memoirs about Beethoven which are, however, extremely interesting; and his account of the great Cavatina from the Quartet Op. 130 has the indubitable ring of truth. In the autumn of 1826 Beethoven went to Gneixendorf near Krems to visit his brother Nikolaus Johann, and there he wrote his last completed work, the *Ersatz* Finale of the String Quartet Op. 135. He was now living in the Schwarzspanierhaus and returned from Gneixendorf to his flat a very ill man.

From the diary of Sir George Smart [original English]:
Friday 9 September 1825:

... At twelve I took Ries to the Hotel Wildemann, the lodgings of Mr. Schlesinger, the music seller of Paris, as I understood from Mr. Holz that Beethoven would be there and there I found him. He received me in the most flattering manner. There was a numerous assembly of professors to hear Beethoven's second new manuscript quartette, bought by Mr. Schlesinger. This quartette is three-quarters of an hour long. They played it twice. The four performers were Schuppanzigh, Holz, Weiss, and Lincke. It is most chromatic and there is a slow movement entitled 'Praise for the recovery of an invalid.' Beethoven intended to allude to himself I suppose for he was very ill during the early part of this year. He directed the performers, and took off his coat the room being warm and crowded. A staccato passage not being expressed to the satisfaction of his eye, for alas, he could not hear, he seized Holz's violin and played the passage a quarter of a tone too flat. I looked over the score during the performance. All paid him the greatest attention. About fourteen were present, those I knew were Boehm (violin), Marx ('cello), Carl Czerny, also Beethoven's nephew, who is like Count St. Antonio, so is Boehm, the violin player. The partner of Steiner, the music-seller, was also there. I fixed to go to Beethoven at Baden on Sunday and left at twenty-five minutes past two.

Leaves from the Journals of Sir George Smart, edited by H. Bertram Cox and C. L. E. Cox, London 1907, p. 108 f.

Carl Holz recalls how, in the spring of 1825, Beethoven talked about his favourite among his works:

For him the crowning achievement of his quartet writing, and his favourite piece, was the E-Flat Cavatina in 3/4 time from the Quartet in B-Flat Major. He actually composed it in tears of melancholy (in the summer of 1825) and confessed to me that his own music had never had such an effect on him before, and that even thinking back to that piece cost him fresh tears.

Kerst II, 187. L. Nohl, *Beethoven*, III, 1867, p. 660.

Dr Gerhard von Breuning on Beethoven's brother Johann:

For several years after the death of the great 'brainowner', his brother, the 'landowner', played a quite singularly naïve rôle. During Ludwig's lifetime, Johann was interested in his brother's works only for the profit that might be realized from them; now, however, he strove to feign

110 Nikolaus Johann, Beethoven's youngest brother, who was a successful apothecary; oil portrait by L. Gross, 1841.

111 Carl Holz, Beethoven's most intimate friend towards the end of his life; miniature by Barbara Frölich-Bogner, 22 February 1824.

the appreciative admirer of those same works. Splendidly bedizened (blue frock-coat, white waistcoat), he would be seated in the front row of the concert hall at performances of his late brother's works; following each one he would shout 'Bravo', his broad mouth wide open, while applauding mightily with his bony hands, clumsily gloved in white.

Breuning 182.

Dr Gerhard von Breuning describes Johann van Beethoven to Alexander Wheelock Thayer:

His hair was blackish brown and combed down smoothly; his hat was well brushed, his clothing clean like that of a man who wants to dress elegantly for Sunday, but more pedantic and awkward, due to his bone structure, which was angular and unattractive. His waist was rather narrow, not a bit of embonpoint; his shoulders were broad; if I recall correctly, he held one shoulder a little lower than the other, or else it was his angular build which made his figure seem somewhat odd. He usually wore a blue frock-coat with brass buttons, a white cravat, white waistcoat, light-coloured breeches, buff-coloured I believe, and cotton gloves, the fingers of which were too long, so that the tips turned

191

over or flopped limply. His hands were broad and bony. His frame was not actually large, but was much larger than Ludwig's. His nose was large and rather long; his eyes were not evenly set, so that one got the impression he had a cast in one eye. His mouth was crooked, one corner was drawn somewhat crookedly upwards, which made him look as though he were smiling mockingly. In his clothing he played the well-to-do dandy, but that did not suit his bony, angular figure. He bore no resemblance whatever to his brother Ludwig.

TDR IV, 264.

From Beethoven's conversation books (about Johann van Beethoven):

[Winter 1822/23]
Count Moritz Lichnowsky: Everyone makes a fool of him; we call him simply 'the Chevalier'. – Everybody says his only merit is that he bears your name.

TDR IV, 264 f.

Ludwig Cramolini, tenor and later producer at the Vienna Court Opera, tells about his last visit to Beethoven:

I saw Beethoven just one more time, at the urging of my mother. It was the 15th or 16th of December 1826. I had already been singing for two years as a tenor at the Imperial and Royal Court Opera and was engaged to be married to Nanette Schechner, an excellent singer. After a performance of *Fidelio*, which Nanny sang and acted beautifully, my mother said, 'I would never have believed the old crosspatch could write such heavenly music, music which quite squeezed the tears out of me.' My mother had never had an opportunity to hear any of Beethoven's music until then. 'You should go call on him; perhaps Beethoven will remember us both. It would be ungrateful of him not to, but I can hardly believe he would be; for someone who feels so deeply, as his composition of *Fidelio* proves he does, must have a kind heart, and I have never doubted that he has.' Nanny also urged me to go, and expressed the desire to make his acquaintance herself on the occasion. I finally agreed, and spoke to Schindler who was then the musical director of the Theater in der Josefstadt, begging him to remind Beethoven of Frau Cramolini's son Louis, who had so often tormented him, but who was now mature enough to recognize and admire his immortal works. A few days later Schindler told me that Beethoven was prepared to receive us, Nanny and me, but we would have to excuse his receiving us lying in bed. We should also bring some music with us, for he wanted to hear or at least see us sing. Thus we drove out to see him on the afternoon of that December day.

When we entered the room the poor man was lying on his sick-bed seriously ill with dropsy. He looked at me, his eyes wide and glowing, then held out his left hand and said, 'So this is young Louis, and already engaged.' Then he nodded to Nanny and said, 'A handsome couple and, so I hear, a couple of able artists too. And how is your dear mother?' He handed us paper and a pencil, and we carried on the ensuing conversation in writing, while he sometimes spoke rather incomprehensibly. Then he asked us to sing for him. Schindler sat down at one of the two pianos that stood side by side in the middle of the room, and we stood facing Beethoven. I wrote that I would sing his 'Adelaide', with which I actually made my initial reputation as a singer. Beethoven nodded affably. But when I tried to begin, my palate and throat had become so dry from anxiety that I could not sing. I asked Schindler to wait a few moments until I could collect myself. Beethoven asked what had happened and why I was not singing, and laughed out loud when Schindler wrote down the reason. Then he said, 'Just sing, dear Louis. Unfortunately I can hear nothing; I only want to see you sing.' Finally I took courage and sang, with true fervour, the song of songs, Beethoven's divine 'Adelaide'. When I finished, Beethoven motioned me over to him, pressed my hand cordially and said, 'From your breathing I can see that you sing correctly, and in your eyes I have read that you feel what you sing. It has been a great pleasure for me.' I was overjoyed at the great man's judgment and had to dry away a tear. When I tried to kiss his hand he withdrew it quickly, saying, 'Kiss the hand of your good mother and remember me often to her, and tell her what a joy it was for me that she still recalls me and has sent her little Louis to see me.'

Then Nanny sang Leonore's aria from *Fidelio*, with such intensity that Beethoven repeatedly began beating time and absolutely devoured her with his wide-open eyes. After the aria, Beethoven held his hand over his eyes for a long while, and then said, 'You are a masterful singer, with a voice possibly somewhat like Milder's, but she did not have the depth of feeling at her command that you do, which showed clearly in your face. What a pity I cannot. . . .' He probably wanted to say 'hear you', but he stopped abruptly and then went on, 'Thank you, Fräulein, for a lovely hour, and may you both be very happy together.' Nanny was also deeply touched and pressed his hand to her heart. There was a short silence. Then Beethoven said, 'But now I feel quite exhausted.'

193

112 Beethoven's study in the Schwarzspanierhaus, where he died; coloured lithograph from a sepia drawing by J. N. Hoechle, *c.* April 1827.

We made ready to go, but before leaving we wrote our thanks and begged his pardon for disturbing him, adding the wish that God might restore him to health soon. With a smile Beethoven said, 'Then I will write an opera for the two of you. My greetings to your father and your dear mother, and if I do regain my health I will ask Schindler to bring them to see me. Adieu my little Louis, and adieu my dear Fidelio.' He pressed our hands again, looked at us sadly but amiably, and finally turned his face to the wall. We went out quietly so as not to disturb him, and were driving back towards town when Nanny broke the silence and said, 'We have probably seen that godlike man for the last time.' The same thought had struck me. I gave Nanny my hand and we wept bitterly.

Kerst II, 217 f. *Frankfurter Zeitung*, No. 270, 29 Sept. 1907.

Ludwig Rellstab on Beethoven's deafness:

[Beethoven:] 'This is a beautiful piano! I got it as a gift from London. Look at the name!' He pointed with his finger to the strip of wood above the keyboard. In fact I saw several names written there which I had not hitherto noticed. There were Moscheles, Kalkbrenner, Cramer, Clementi, Broadwood himself. The circumstance was an impressive one. The wealthy, artistically minded manufacturer could not have found a worthier object on whom to bestow an instrument, which he seems to have found particularly successful, than on Beethoven. The afore-mentioned great artists had reverently signed their names, as it were, rather like godparents; and thus the peculiar remembrance-book travelled far across the seas and was laid at the feet of the highest and most famous as a token of honour from those famous men. 'It is a wonderful present,' said Beethoven looking at me, 'and it has a beautiful tone,' he continued turning towards the piano without taking his eyes off me. He struck a chord softly. Never will another chord pierce me to the quick with such sadness and heartbreak. He has played C major in the right hand and B natural in the bass; he looked at me steadily and repeated the false chord several times to let the mild tone of the instrument sound, and the greatest musician on earth could not hear the dissonance!
Kerst II, 136f.

Anton Schindler on Carl Holz:

Carl Holz was a respectable man who had studied the classics and who had a good knowledge of music, the latter borne out by his place in the quartet association that has gone down in musical history. But Carl Holz was every inch a Viennese 'Phaeacian' and of the first water, too, towards which class our Beethoven had always revealed a deeply-rooted antipathy; nor was it in his nature for him to overlook it. The young man was, however, quite an excellent mathematician, and it was this quality alone which made Beethoven overlook both the Phaeacian and the musician. For with his dual personality Beethoven needed such a specialist in the same way that Wallenstein needed the astrologer Seni. . . .

Noticeable were not only the buffooneries which Carl Holz had written in his own hand, not the frequent attacks on very highly placed persons and others, but rather the high degree of inner irritability in which the master was henceforth kept, and in which state he was obviously pleased with himself. The divergence from old, deeply-rooted principles even revealed itself in Beethoven's accompanying his young friend to gatherings of utter strangers in public places, taverns and wine-shops, and to the shops of music-dealers favoured by him. This did not fail to cause a stir. C. Holz seemed intent on proving that he could do anything with the otherwise retiring composer and subject him to his will. And truly he was able to achieve the unbelievable. Does one need stronger evidence of this than the fact that Beethoven, in the midst of all the frenzy of speculation in which he found himself at the time, stood godfather to his new friend's first-born son? This revealed that our master's mind was in a state of metamorphosis that dumbfounded those who thought that they knew him. It is unfortunately true that under such guidance sacrifices were sometimes made to Bacchus – before the eyes of strangers; precisely this increased the regret of all true friends and disciples. Dr. Wawruch's accusing words, 'sedebat et bibebat,' refer to this association only. The period of these excesses extended, thank heaven, only from the autumn of 1825 until the summer of 1826.

Schindler II, 108 ff.

Fanny Linzbauer on Carl Holz's last visit to Beethoven:

'Haslinger, Castelli and I went to see him. All three of us knelt at his bedside.' – Holz's voice failed him, he covered his face and wept. – 'He blessed us,' he said with great effort, 'and we kissed his hand and never saw him again!'

Kerst II, 216 f.

From Beethoven's conversation books:

[End of February 1827]
Young Breuning: No one can stand Holz; all who know him say he is deceitful. He acts as though he likes you, God knows how much. –

He is very able at shamming. –

He can lie like a book. –

You are the best of all, the others are all scoundrels. –

If you were not so good-natured you could ask him to pay for his board, and with good reason. –

He likes your wine best of all. –

Schindler: I gave Herr Holz a good piece of my mind yesterday. –

The result was that he was quite courteous when he left. –

I heard that he let it be known somewhere that he does not like my coming to see you. –

I called him to account for that, but he insisted he had not said anything whatever about jealousy of that kind. He said he must divide his time between his office, his lessons and his bride, and cannot come to see you for that reason. –

[*A later holograph note by Schindler:* It must be stated here that it was Herr Holz and no one else who openly said everywhere that Beethoven had contracted dropsy purely as a result of too much wine-drinking. This is how the belief spread that he was a drinker. The truth is that Herr Holz, who was a heavy drinker himself, often induced our Beethoven to drink more than usual. But thank heaven that this period, during which he let himself be led about by Herr Holz and drank a great deal, lasted approximately 18 months only, from the early summer of 1825 until the end of September 1826.]
Kerst II, 307 f.

Dr Gerhard von Breuning on Carl van Beethoven:
The time for examinations at the Technical Institute came, and there were again debts to be settled. Time was pressing, and Carl, prepared neither in knowledge nor in pocket, and fearing his uncle's reproaches more and more (he was 'tired of them long since' and found them 'absurd'), decided to make a change; not for the better, as his uncle longed for him to do, but for the worse, by killing himself. He bought two pistols, drove to Baden and climbed the tower of the ruins of Rauhenstein Castle. Once at the top, he put both pistols to his temples and fired. He wounded himself only superficially – the periosteum was injured – but he still had to be taken to the *Allgemeines Krankenhaus* [General Hospital] in Vienna.

Beethoven was badly shaken by the news. His grief at this event was indescribable; he was as despondent as a father who has lost his adored son. My mother met him on the Glacis looking quite stricken. 'Do you know what has happened to me? My Carl has shot himself!' – 'And is he dead?' 'No, he only grazed himself. He is still alive, and there are hopes of saving him. But the disgrace he has brought on me – and I loved him so much. . . . – '

The surgeon Ignaz Seng, who died as recently as 16 September 1879, told me the following account of his meeting Beethoven: 'I was *Secundarius* at the *Allgemeines Krankenhaus* in Vienna, working in the surgical clinic headed by *Primarius* Gassner, a part of which was the so-called 3-Gulden floor; I lived to the left of the large courtyard facing the middle

113 Carl van Beethoven; anonymous miniature (original disappeared). This son of Beethoven's brother Carl Anton Caspar caused the composer endless anxiety but was the object of his possessive love.

house, on the ground floor of which the administrative offices were located. In the late summer of 1826, on a day when I had inspection duty, a man dressed in a grey coat came up to me. I thought at first he was just an ordinary burgher. He asked coolly, "Are you *Herr Secundarius* Seng? They told me at the reception office that I should see you. Is my nephew one of your patients, that wretch, that scoundrel, etc.?" After asking the patient's name, I said he was, and added that he was in a room on the 3-Gulden floor, had been treated for a gunshot wound, and did he want to see him?, at which he answered, "I am Beethoven." And while I led him to his nephew, he went on speaking: "I actually did not want to visit him because he does not deserve it. He has caused me too much annoyance, but. . . ." And he went on talking about the catastrophe and about his nephew's behaviour, and how he spoiled him too much, and so on. I was quite astonished to have, beneath that outward appearance, the great Beethoven before me, and promised him I would do everything to look after his nephew.'
Breuning 119 ff.

From Beethoven's conversation books:

[Summer 1826]
Carl: Dearest father, you can be certain that the sorrow I have brought you causes me more grief than you. Fear has restored my reason, and I now see what I have done. If I thought that you believe I did it deliberately, I would be inconsolable. It happened in a state of drunkenness. If you can forgive me, I promise you I will never touch another drop of wine, so that I do not lapse into that condition again. But it causes me great pain to know that you can think such things about me. What sort of

person would I be if I had even the remotest intention of causing you grief? Forgive me just this once more! I will certainly not drink wine any more; that was the cause of everything; I could not restrain myself and did not know where I was. I beg you once more, forgive me!
Kerst II, 304.

Ferdinand Hiller visits the ailing Beethoven with Hummel and his wife:

[8 March 1827]

We drove out to the suburb. We walked through a large anteroom in which stood high cupboards holding thick bundles of music tied with string, and then entered Beethoven's sitting room and were not a little amazed to find the master sitting, apparently quite comfortably, at the window. He wore a long, grey dressing-gown, which at that moment was completely open, and high boots up to the knee. Emaciated from his serious illness, he seemed tall when he stood up; he was unshaven, and his hair fell in disorderly fashion about his temples. The expression on his face became friendly and bright when he saw Hummel, and he seemed as exceptionally pleased at seeing Hummel as Hummel was to see him. The two men embraced warmly. Hummel introduced me; Beethoven was quite gracious towards me, and I was made to sit opposite him by the window. It is known that conversation with Beethoven had in part to be written; he spoke, but those with whom he spoke had to write down their questions and answers. For this purpose thick booklets of normal quarto writing paper and pencils were always close at hand. . . . Beethoven followed the writer's hand with eager eyes, and took in the written words at a glance rather than reading them. The liveliness of the conversation of course suffered greatly by the visitor's having constantly to write. . . . At the start the conversation, as was customary, concerned household affairs, the journey and our stay, my connection with Hummel and such things. Beethoven asked after Goethe's health with unusual concern, and we were able to report that all was well. As to his own health, Beethoven complained greatly. 'I have lain about for four months already,' he exclaimed, 'and one's patience finally wears out!' – In addition to that, there was much about Vienna that was not to his liking, and he spoke bitingly about the 'present taste in art' and the 'dilettantism that is ruining everything here.' Nor was the government spared, even its highest representatives. 'Write a bookful of penitential songs and dedicate it to the Empress,' he said to Hummel with an ill-humoured laugh; but Hummel made no use of that well-intentioned advice.

[13 March 1827]

We found his condition appreciably worsened. He lay in bed, seemed to be in pain and groaned at times, but spoke much and animatedly despite it. He seemed now to regret that he had not married, and at our first visit he had joked with Hummel about it. . . . 'You', he said this time, 'are a lucky fellow; you have a wife who looks after you, who loves you – but poor me!' And he gave a deep sigh. He also begged Hummel to bring his wife again; she had not come, for she could not bring herself to see, in such a state, a man she had known at the height of his powers. A short time before, he had been given a picture of the house in which Haydn was born; he had it near the bed and showed it to us. 'I was happy as a child to receive it,' he said, 'the cradle of a great man!' He also asked a favour of Hummel with regard to Schindler, whose name has been mentioned so often subsequently. 'He is a good fellow,' he said, 'and has done quite a lot for me. He is to give a concert soon, and I promised I would take part in it. But nothing will come of that now. I would like you to do me the favour of playing. One has to help poor artists to get on.' Hummel of course said he would.

Visit of 20 March: 'I will probably be up above soon,' he whispered after greeting us. He made other similar exclamations. He spoke of his plans and prospects and announced his intention of making a journey to London as soon as he was better, to show his gratitude to the English for their gift. 'I will compose a big overture and a symphony for them,' he said. And then he wanted to visit Frau Hummel and stay for a time in various places. His eyes, still quite full of life at Hummel's last visit, dimmed today, and he had difficulty from time to time in sitting up.

March 26: While I was in convivial company at the home of the musical amateur Herr von Liebenberg [a former pupil of Hummel's], guests arrived with the news that Ludwig van Beethoven was no longer alive; he had died at about 5:45.

On Thursday, 29 March, the funeral was held. We gathered at the lodgings of the deceased. . . . From there the cortège began moving towards the *Dreifaltigkeitskirche* [Church of the Trinity] at about 3 o'clock. Eight Kapellmeister, Eibler, Hummel, Seyfried, Kreutzer, Weigl, Gyrowetz, Würfel and Gänsbacher were the pall-bearers. . . . I could not get into the church, but I drove from there with Hummel to the Währing Cemetery, which was crowded with people. . . . The coffin was lowered into the earth; deeply moved, Hummel threw some laurel wreaths after it; others followed. . . .

K. Benyovszky, *J. N. Hummel, Der Mensch und Künstler*, Bratislava 1934, pp. 151 ff.

Letter from Anton Schindler to Ignaz Moscheles:

Vienna, 24 March 1827

. . . My dear Moscheles, when you read these lines our friend will no longer be among the living. His death is approaching rapidly, and all of us wish only to see him released from his terrible suffering. There is nothing else left to hope for. For a week he has lain as though almost dead, but has pulled his remaining strength together now and again to put a question or to ask for something. His condition is terrible and exactly like that of the Duke of York, about which we read recently. He is in a permanent state of dull brooding; his head hangs forward onto his breast and he stares fixedly at one spot for hours; he seldom recognizes his closest acquaintances unless he is told who they are. In short, it is dreadful to see. This condition can last just a few days more, for all bodily functions have ceased since yesterday. So if God will, he is soon released, and we with him. People have begun to come in droves to have a last look, although no one is admitted except for those who are so impudent as to badger a dying man in his final hours.

Apart from a few words at the beginning, he dictated the letter to you word for word; it is probably the last of his life, although he whispered the words 'Smart – Stumpff – write' disjointedly to me today. If he can still write so much as his name, I will see that it is done. – He knows the end is coming, for he said to Herr von Breuning and me yesterday, 'Plaudite, amici, comoedia finita est!' Yesterday we were also able to put his testament in order, although there is nothing but a few old pieces of furniture and manuscripts. He was at work on a string quintet and his tenth symphony, which he mentions in his letter to you. Two movements of the quintet are finished. It was intended for Diabelli. –
Kerst II, 222 f.

The last testament:

prs. 29 March 1827.

My nephew Karl shall be my sole heir; the capital of my estate, however, shall go to his natural or testamentary heirs. –

Vienna, 23 March 1827.
Ludwig van Beethoven mp.

TDR V, 485.

Professor Dr Wawruch's medical report on Beethoven's final illness:

. . . During January, February and March, emaciation increased rapidly and there was a considerable loss in vital power. In dejected moments

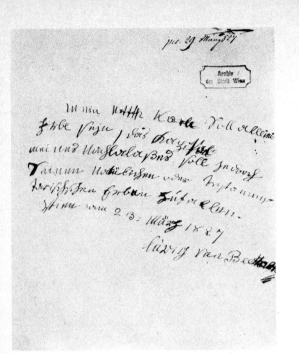

114 Beethoven's last will of 23 March 1827 making his nephew Carl sole beneficiary.

115, 116 Beethoven in a coma; both drawings by J. E. Teltscher.

following the fourth puncture, Beethoven prognosticated his approaching death, and he was not mistaken. No words had the power to console him any longer, and when I told him that the coming spring weather would alleviate his suffering he answered me with a smile, 'My day's work is done; if there were a physician who could still help, [the next words in English] his name shall be called wonderful!' – This distressing reference to Handel's *Messiah* affected me so greatly that I, deeply moved, was forced to confirm silently the truth of those words.

The fatal day drew nearer. My professional obligations as a physician, so gratifying and yet at times so grievous, demanded that I draw my suffering friend's attention to it, so that he could meet his civil and religious obligations. With the tenderest consideration, I wrote the words of admonition on a sheet of paper (for we had long been able to communicate only in this way). Beethoven read the writing with unparalleled composure, slowly and pensively, his face as though transfigured; he gave me his hand gravely and warmly, and said, 'Let the priest come.' Then he became quiet and thoughtful and nodded to me kindly, 'I will see you again soon.' Shortly thereafter, Beethoven performed his devotions with meek submission and turned to the friends standing about him with the words, 'Plaudite amici, finita est comoedia!'

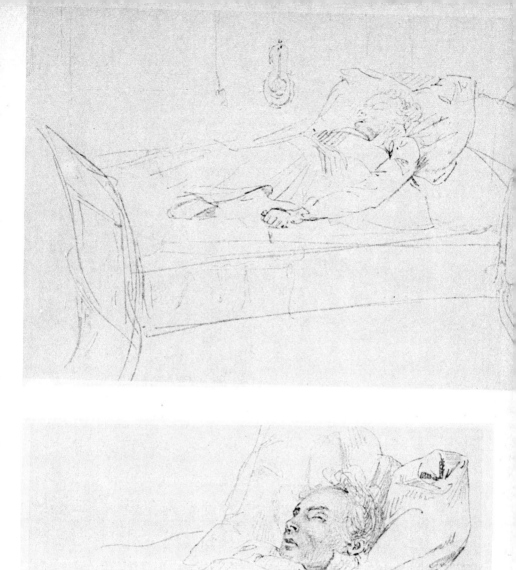

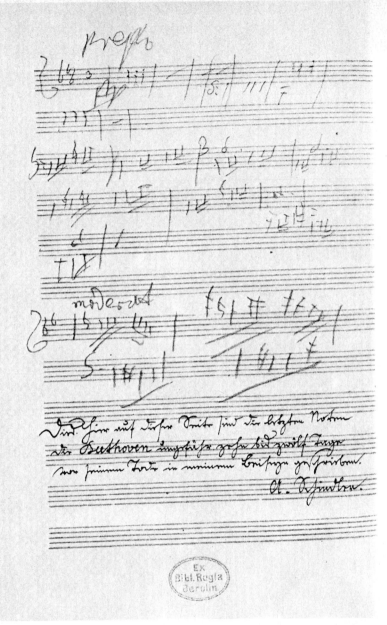

117 Autograph of the last music Beethoven wrote, sketches for the Tenth Symphony.

A few hours later he lost consciousness, lapsed into a coma and the death rattle began in his throat. The next morning all symptoms of the approaching end were present. The 26th of March was stormy and dull; towards 6 in the afternoon a snowstorm began, accompanied by thunder and lightning. – Beethoven died. – What would a Roman augur have concluded about his apotheosis from the fortuitous unrest of the elements?

Kerst II, 214 f.

From the Diaries of Joseph Carl Rosenbaum:

Monday, 26 March 1827: freezing, snow flurries, north wind. . . . After 4 o'clock the sky grew darker; snowstorm and thunder and lightning. A revolution in nature; three violent thunderclaps followed. Bab. Beck's funeral at the same hour. . . . Death of Ludwig van Bethowen about 6 o'clock, of dropsy of the abdomen, aged 56. He is no more! His name lives in the light of glory.

Wednesday, 28 March 1827: Changeable, not so cold. . . . At Haslinger's I spoke with Steiner about Bethowen's will; he left 7 bank shares and 1,000 Florins from London in trust for his dissolute nephew the cadet. A string quartet was his swansong. – Haslinger published an invitation to the funeral.

Autograph. Österreichische Nationalbibliothek, Handschriftensammlung.

Anselm Hüttenbrenner writes about Beethoven's death:

When I entered Beethoven's bedroom just before 3 o'clock on the afternoon of 26 March 1827, I found Breuning, his son and Frau van Beethoven, the wife of Johann van Beethoven, landowner and apothecary from Linz, and also my friend Joseph Teltscher, the portraitist. I believe Professor Schindler was also present. After a time the aforementioned gentlemen left the composer, who was in the throes of death, and harboured little hope of finding him still alive on their return.

During Beethoven's last moments there was no one present in the death-chamber but Frau van Beethoven and myself. Beethoven lay in the final agony, unconscious and with the death-rattle in his throat, from 3 o'clock, when I arrived, until after 5 o'clock; then there was suddenly a loud clap of thunder accompanied by a bolt of lightning which illuminated the death-chamber with a harsh light (there was snow in front of Beethoven's house). After this unexpected natural phenomenon, which had shaken me greatly, Beethoven opened his eyes, raised his right hand and, his fist clenched, looked upwards for several seconds

118 Beethoven on his deathbed; lithograph by Joseph Danhauser from his own drawing.

with a very grave, threatening countenance, as though to say, 'I defy you, powers of evil! Away! God is with me.' It also seemed as though he were calling like a valiant commander to his faint-hearted troops: 'Courage, men! Forward! Trust in me! The victory is ours!'

As he let his hand sink down onto the bed again, his eyes half closed. My right hand lay under his head, my left hand rested on his breast. There was no more breathing, no more heartbeat! The great composer's spirit fled from this world of deception into the kingdom of truth. I shut the half-open eyes of the deceased, kissed them, and then his forehead, mouth and hands. At my request Frau van Beethoven cut a lock of his hair and gave it to me as a sacred relic of Beethoven's last hour.

Kerst II, 232 f. (Hüttenbrenner published this report in the Graz *Tagespost* of 23 October 1868.)

Beethoven's funeral was an enormous affair in which thousands of people took part. The poet Franz Grillparzer wrote the funeral oration and summed up the general sense of mourning that late afternoon in March 1827.

Description of Beethoven's funeral from Landau's Erstes poetisches Beethoven-Album *(Prague 1877):*

Vienna, 29 March 1827.

His friends had scarcely performed, with grieving hearts, their last kind offices for him, when they united to hold the funeral, which was set for the afternoon of 29 March due to the preparations that would have to be made. Invitations were immediately printed and sent out in large numbers. The lovely, warm spring day attracted a huge crowd of curious people to the Glacis of the Alser district beyond the Schottentor, to the so-called Schwarzspanier House where Beethoven had lived; and the throng produced by the confluence of some 20,000 people of all classes and vocations finally increased to such proportions that the gates of the house had to be shut, for the courtyard where the body lay in state, although large, could not accommodate any more of the closely pressed crowd. The clergy appeared at about 3:30 o'clock and the cortège then began to move. Although the distance to the church is scarcely 500 paces in a straight line, it took nearly 1½ hours for the cortège to reach it, for it had to move extremely slowly through the surging throng, which could not be kept in check except by force. Eight singers from the Imperial and Royal Court Opera carried the coffin; before they shouldered it, however, they sang the chorale by B. A. Weber from *Wilhelm Tell.* After that all the mourners, colleagues of the deceased, friends and admirers of his sublime genius, poets, actors, musicians and many more arranged themselves in line; all were dressed in full mourning, with black gloves, fluttering crape-bands, sprays of white lilies in their left arm and flambeaus wound about with crape. Following the cross-bearer who led the cortège, there came four trombonists and 16 of Vienna's best singers; they played and sang alternately the *Miserere mei Deus,* the melody of which had been composed by the deceased master. He had been staying with his brother in Linz in the late autumn of 1812, and Glöggl, the cathedral Kapellmeister there, had asked him for a few short settings for trombones for his town musicians, to be used on All Souls' Day. Beethoven wrote a so-called *Equale a quatro Tromboni,* true to the venerable old style and marked by the originality of his bold harmonic structure. From this brass quartet, Kapellmeister von Seyfried made, quite in the spirit of the composer of those grave and

119 Beethoven's funeral procession, attended by some 20,000 people; watercolour by Franz Stöber.

pious funerary pieces, a four-part vocal chorus to words from the Psalms; excellently sung in alternation with the muffled resounding trombones, it produced an awesome moving effect. The priests followed, and then came the splendidly ornate bier, flanked by the Kapellmeister Eybler, Hummel, Seyfried and Kreutzer on the right and Weigl, Gyrowetz, Gänsbacher and Würfel on the left; they held the hanging white ribbons and were accompanied on both sides by torch-bearers, among whom were Castelli, Grillparzer, Bernard, Anschütz, Böhm, Czerny, Lablache, David, Pacini, Rodicchi, Meric, Mayseder, Merk, Lannoy, Linke, Riotto, Schubert, Weidmann, Weiss, Schuppanzigh and many others.

At the end of the cortège came the pupils of the Conservatory, the St Anne's music students, the most distinguished persons of rank, e.g. Count Moritz von Dietrichstein, Councillor von Mosel and Councillor von Breuning (the latter a childhood friend of the deceased and the executor of his will), and many others.

Arriving at the church, the body was blessed at the high altar, during which ceremony the 16-voice male choir sang the hymn *Libera me, Domine, de morte aeterna* composed by Seyfried in *Stylo alto* [*vecchio*]. As the hearse, drawn by four horses, carried the composer's mortal remains to the cemetery beyond the Linie, it was accompanied by 200 coaches. At the gates of the cemetery Anschütz spoke, full of inspiration and emotion, the incomparably beautiful funeral oration written by Grillparzer; its deep sentiment and the masterly delivery of it touched all hearts, and many a tear flowed from noble eyes in honour of the deceased prince of composers. Several hundred copies of two poems by Castelli and von Schlechta were distributed among the company. After the coffin had been lowered into the ground, and three laurel wreaths with it, the mourners, deeply moved, left the sacred resting-place as twilight began to fall.

Kerst II, 237 ff.

Franz Grillparzer's funeral oration:

We who stand here at the grave of the deceased are in a sense the representatives of an entire nation, the whole German people, come to mourn the passing of one celebrated half of that which remained to us from the vanished brilliance of the art of our homeland, of the spiritual efflores-

120 Franz Grillparzer; watercolour by M. M. Daffinger, 1827. The great Austrian poet, who had known Beethoven personally since 1805, wrote the funeral oration.

cence of the fatherland. The hero of poetry in the German language and tongue still lives – and long may he live. But the last master of resounding song, the gracious mouth by which music spoke, the man who inherited and increased the immortal fame of Handel and Bach, of Haydn and Mozart, has ceased to be; and we stand weeping over the broken strings of an instrument now stilled.

An instrument now stilled. Let me call him that! For he was an artist, and what he was, he was only through art. The thorns of life had wounded him deeply, and as the shipwrecked man clutches the saving shore, he flew to your arms, oh wondrous sister of the good and true, comforter in affliction, the art that comes from on high! He held fast to you, and even when the gate through which you had entered was shut, you spoke through a deafened ear to him who could no longer discern you; and he carried your image in his heart, and when he died it still lay on his breast.

He was an artist, and who shall stand beside him? As the behemoth sweeps through the seas, he swept across the boundaries of his art. From the cooing of the dove to the thunder's roll, from the subtlest interweaving of wilful artifices to that awesome point at which the fabric passes over into the lawlessness of clashing natural forces – he traversed all, he comprehended everything. He who follows him cannot continue; he must begin anew, for his predecessor ended only where art ends.

Adelaide and Leonore! Commemoration of the heroes of Vittoria and humble tones of the Mass! Offspring of three and four-part voices. Resounding symphony, 'Freude, schöner Götterfunken', the swansong. Muses of song and of strings, gather at his grave and strew it with laurel!

He was an artist, but also a man, a man in every sense, in the highest sense. Because he shut himself off from the world, they called him hostile; and callous, because he shunned feelings. Oh, he who knows he is hardened does not flee! (It is the most delicate point that is most easily blunted, that bends or breaks.)

The excess of feeling avoids feelings. He fled the world because he did not find, in the whole compass of his loving nature, a weapon with which to resist it. He withdrew from his fellow-men after he had given them everything and had received nothing in return. He remained alone because he found no second self. But until his death he preserved a human heart for all men, a father's heart for his own people, the whole world.

Thus he was, thus he died, thus will he live for all time!

And you who have followed our escort to this place, hold your sorrow in sway. You have not lost him but have won him. No living man enters the halls of immortality. The body must die before the gates are opened. He whom you mourn is now among the greatest men of all time, unassailable for ever. Return to your homes, then, distressed but composed. And whenever, during your lives, the power of his works overwhelms you like a coming storm; when your rapture pours out in the midst of a generation yet unborn; then remember this hour and think: we were there when they buried him, and when he died we wept!
Kerst II, 250f.

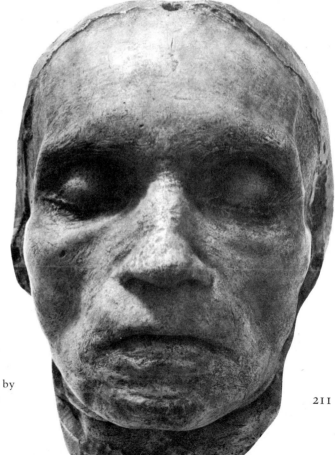

121 Beethoven's death-mask, by
Joseph Danhauser (see ill. 14).

Sources of illustrations

Index